JESSE OWENS

Other titles in the *African-American Biography Library*

JESSE OWENS

"I Always Loved Running"

Jeff Burlingame

Series Consultant:
Dr. Russell L. Adams,
Emeritus Professor,
Howard University

Enslow Publishers, Inc.
40 Industrial Road
Box 398
Berkeley Heights, NJ 07922
USA
http://www.enslow.com

Library of Congress Cataloging-in-Publication Data

Burlingame, Jeff.
    Jesse Owens : "I always loved running" / Jeff Burlingame.
      p. cm. — (African-American biography library)
    Includes bibliographical references and index.
    Summary: "Explores the life of Jesse Owens, including his childhood and family, his rise
to excellence in track and field, his 1936 Olympic triumph, and his death and legacy"—
Provided by publisher.
    ISBN 978-0-7660-3497-6
    1. Owens, Jesse, 1913—Juvenile literature. 2. Track and field athletes—United
States—Biography—Juvenile literature. 3. African American track and field athletes—
Biography—Juvenile literature. I. Title.
GV697.O9B87 2010
796.42092—dc22
[B]   2010015697

Printed in the United States of America

10 9 8 7 6 5 4 3 2 1

102010 Lake Book Manufacturing, Inc., Melrose Park, IL

To Our Readers: We have done our best to make sure all Internet Addresses in this book were
active and appropriate when we went to press. However, the author and the publisher have
no control over and assume no liability for the material available on those Internet sites or
on other Web sites they may link to. Any comments or suggestions can be sent by e-mail to
comments@enslow.com or to the address on the back cover.

♻ Enslow Publishers, Inc., is committed to printing our books on recycled paper. The paper in
every book contains 10% to 30% post-consumer waste (PCW). The cover board on the outside
of each book contains 100% PCW. Our goal is to do our part to help young people and the
environment too!

Illustration Credits: Associated Press, pp. 10, 12, 49, 51, 63, 72, 79, 84, 98, 102, 109, 111;
The Granger Collection, New York, p. 24; © histopics / ullstein bild / The Image Works, p. 6;
Hulton Archive / Getty Images, p. 66; © Jeff Greenberg / The Image Works, p. 18; Keystone
/ Eyedea / Everett Collection, pp. 35, 56; Mary Evans Picture Library / Everett Collection,
p. 68; Michael Dalder / Reuters / Landov, p. 114; Special Collections, Michael Schwartz Library
at Cleveland State University, p. 22; The Ohio State University Photo Archives, pp. 5, 7, 14, 27,
30, 32, 40, 43, 46, 54, 58, 75, 81, 86, 88, 92, 94, 96, 105, 108.

Cover Illustration: Library of Congress (Jesse Owens running at the 1936 Olympics);
The Ohio State University Photo Archives (Portrait of Jesse Owens).

Contents

Jesse Owens

Chapter 1

A Historic Triumph

More than 110,000 people watched from the stands as the runners gathered at the starting line. As each of the six men dug their shoes into the soggy cinder track, the enormous crowd at Olympic Stadium in Berlin, Germany, began to buzz with anticipation. These were the six fastest runners in the world, and it was time for the finals of the Olympic 100-meter dash. As one of the most basic and exciting Olympic events, the 100 meters has always been a crowd favorite. It was the event everyone wanted to see. This year, 1936, American Jesse Owens was the one most people wanted to watch run the race.

The twenty-two-year-old college student from Ohio State University appeared to be unbeatable. He had wowed everyone in his preliminary races. In one the day before, he had tied the world record of 10.3 seconds. The record already was his; he had set it earlier in the year. In the next heat, Owens broke the world record by running 10.2 seconds, only to soon find out the record would not stand because there had been too much wind at his back during the race. At least that is what the German officials ruled, even after American photographers produced pictures that showed the stadium's flags were not blowing at all.[1]

Earlier on this day, August 3, Owens had dominated his semifinal race. This set the stage for a thrilling final that evening. The winner of the 100-meter dash would earn the title of "World's Fastest Man." As it was in every Olympic event, a gold medal also awaited the winner. Its winner often gained immense popularity and notoriety world-wide. But this race was even more special than any others. It offered a special twist. This was Germany's Olympics, and Germany's ruler, Adolf Hitler, believed blacks were an inferior race. Two black runners had made it to the finals, and Owens was one of them. Needless to say, Hitler did not want Owens to win. He was cheering for his fellow German, Erich Borchmeyer. Hitler believed his German athletes were superior and could not be beaten.

As Owens, Borchmeyer, and the four other runners dug their feet into the track's soft surface and crouched into their starting positions, the German starter barked his orders:

Auf die Pläze! On your marks! Owens took a deep breath, swallowed hard, and focused his eyes toward the finish line.

Fertig! Get set! Owens rose from his crouch, ready to spring forward at the next signal . . .

Bang! At the blast of the starter's gun, Owens burst from the starting holes he had dug just moments earlier. His start was perfect. Within ten strides, he had opened up a large lead over the rest of the field. As he cruised down the wet track in the inside lane, his lead grew larger. Near the end of the race, fellow American Ralph Metcalfe somewhat closed the gap. But Metcalfe had faltered a bit at the start and, by that point, Owens's winning was a formality. Owens broke the tape in 10.3 seconds, tying the Olympic record. Hitler's pick, the German Borchmeyer, finished a distant fifth.

A majority of the packed stadium erupted with joy at Owens's accomplishment. They had hoped for their countryman to pull off an upset but knew his chances were slim. Owens was simply too dominating, and the crowd appreciated the greatness it was witnessing. Owens had again tied the Olympic and world records and did not even look very tired at

> Owens was simply too dominating, and the crowd appreciated the greatness it was witnessing.

Jesse Owens (at far right crossing the finish line) is shown
winning the 100-meter dash at the 1936 Olympics. Owens
ran the race in 10.3 seconds, tying the Olympic record.

the end of the race. The mostly German crowd began
wildly chanting his name:

Yess-say Oh-vens! . . . Yess-say Oh-vens!

Throughout the rest of the Olympics, the crowd kept
chanting Owens's name. It was the same reaction he had
received since arriving in Berlin. People stood outside his
bedroom window at the Olympic Village trying to snap a
photo of him. Owens was an international superstar. One
newspaper reported, "The autograph maniacs grabbed

him and twisted him around and people poked the snouts of cameras into his face."[2]

Hitler was appalled by Owens's accomplishment. In a little more than ten seconds, he had seen a black man win the hearts of his followers and defeat one of his "superior" athletes. It was a low point for the German leader.

On the first day of the Olympics, Hitler had shaken the hands of most of the gold medalists to congratulate them. But, on this day, he would not shake Owens's hand or meet with the champion, even after one official encouraged him to do so. Hitler said, "The Americans should have been ashamed of themselves for allowing their medals to be won by Negroes. I would never have shaken this Negro's hand. . . . Do you really think I'd allow myself to be photographed shaking hands with a Negro?"[3]

The day before Owens's win in the 100 meters, Hitler also had not congratulated the winners of the high jump event, which included two African Americans. Some historians argue that timing may have been the reason he did not do so—because Hitler had left the stadium shortly after his country's jumpers were eliminated. Others say Hitler had decided after the first day that he would not congratulate any winners in public because it was too time consuming, and that is why he did not congratulate Owens. But to this day, most believe Hitler refused to shake Owens's hand because he was black.

If it occurred, Owens did not seem to mind the rebuke from Hitler. In fact, he may not even have believed that

Adolf Hitler (center) watches track and field events at the Olympic Stadium during the Olympic Games. Hitler refused to congratulate Jesse Owens after his victory.

it happened. As he told the story sometime later, he said, "When I passed [Hitler] he arose, waved his hand at me, and I waved back at him."[4] Some historians believe Owens had imagined the wave, or was making it up for various reasons. But as the years wore on, Owens began to go along with the stories of how Hitler had refused to shake his hand. The story became legendary. In a book he wrote in 1970, Owens said, "Hitler treated me as if I were some kind of animal."[5]

At the time and even today, the negative version of the story prevailed, and newspapers printed such headlines as "Hitler Snubs Jesse!"[6] and "Owens Humiliated in Hitler's Land."[7] Regardless of whether or not Hitler had refused to shake Owens's hand, a black man from the United States had shattered the German leader's idea of what these Olympics would be. Hitler had hoped the games would be a showcase for what he thought was a superior race of humans, the "Aryans." In Hitler's perfect world, his pure-blooded German athletes—many who were blond haired and blue eyed—would have dominated every event. It did not turn out that way.

For the rest of the Olympics, Owens continued with his mission. He had other events to compete in, more records to set, and an entire country to represent. He had no idea that what he accomplished over the next several days would forever change his life. He had no idea what impact the ten seconds he spent blazing down the wet Berlin track would have on history. He had no idea what devastation the German leader who had refused to shake his hand soon would wreak upon the world.

In the days and decades to come, people across the world would read and write about Owens's life story. They would applaud at how he had overshadowed an evil, glory-seeking dictator and marvel at how he had overcome tremendous odds to even have had the chance to do so.

Chapter 2

A Love for Running

From the beginning, the odds of succeeding at anything in life were against James Cleveland Owens. In fact, the odds were against his entire family and every other black person who lived in the vicinity of Oakville, the hilly northern Alabama community where J.C., as his parents called him, was born on September 12, 1913. J.C.'s parents, Henry and Emma Alexander Owens, were poor sharecroppers whose ancestors had come from Africa as slaves.

In Alabama, the Owenses farmed the land owned by another person and received half of the crop they had produced. After the crop was harvested, the Owenses sold their share and used the money to pay for basic needs. Many seasons, it was a struggle to survive, especially when bad weather caused the crops to fail or not produce as well as had been hoped. Oftentimes, Henry Owens and his children would hunt small animals, such as rabbits, to help feed the family. They also fished the nearby pond. The family had a small garden that grew beans, onions, and tomatoes.

J.C.'s ancestors had come to America from Africa in the 1830s as slaves and took their surname of Owens from their slave owner.[1] When J.C. was born, his family was working on a section of land owned by a white man named Albert Owens. They then moved to a larger farm to work for a man named John Clannon. J.C. was the Owens's ninth and next-to-last child. He had five brothers and four sisters. Each of the children helped on the farm—all of them except J.C., that is, because, from an early age, he often was sick, especially during the cold winter months, when the freezing wind would blow through the gaps in the walls of the family's small wooden shack. Years later, J.C. remembered, "I was the only one who couldn't help, not because I was too young but because I was too sick. Every winter for as long as I can remember, I'd come down with pneumonia. A couple of those years, I was close to never seeing spring."[2] His mother had a name for her son's sickness. She called it the "Devil's Cold."

> "I was the only one who couldn't help, not because I was too young but because I was too sick."

Sharecropping

When the American Civil War ended in 1865, enslaved African Americans throughout the United States were freed, thanks to the passage of the Thirteenth Amendment of the United States Constitution. In the South, many of those former slaves had spent their entire lives working for white plantation owners, tending to their land and harvesting their crops. As slaves, the workers had been forced to work for free. But as free men and women, this would no longer be the case. Because the plantation owners still needed workers and the recently freed slaves needed to make money to survive, the system of sharecropping was developed.

Sharecropping was an agreement between the former slaves and the white landowners that allowed families to continue working the land. But as sharecroppers, they would receive a portion of the profits after the crop was harvested and sold. The system was not perfect by any means. Landowners charged sharecroppers for the use of equipment and other goods and subtracted that from any money they were paid after the crops—most often cotton—were sold. At the end of each season, black families often received no money for an entire year's work. Defeated and feeling hopeless, the sharecroppers would repeat the cycle the following year. In the 1930s, machines eventually replaced much of the work black families had been doing on the farms and helped put an end to sharecropping. By that time, many blacks had moved on to other jobs or to other parts of the country, seeking wealth and an easier life.

The skinny, undernourished kid had other health problems, as well. When J.C. was five, he discovered a lump on his chest. When he showed his mother, she decided it needed to be removed. The closest doctor was miles away and was too expensive for the Owens family to afford anyway, so Emma Owens decided to do the surgery herself. It was not the first lump she had removed from her young son's body. But this one was the worst yet. The lump went deep into J.C.'s chest near his heart, and his mom carved it out with a sterile knife. For days, J.C. bled and was in immense pain, but he survived the surgery. J.C. later said the experience helped him in many ways. In his autobiography, he wrote: " . . . the 'cutting' turned out to be a real good thing for me. Not only because that bump would have crippled me, whatever it was, but also because from that day on, no physical hurt or discomfort made much of an impression on me."[3]

By the next year, J.C. was healthy enough to walk to the building that served as both the community's school and its Baptist church. The one-room building was nine miles from their farm, but that is where J.C. had to go every day if he wanted to get an education. On Sundays, the family would dress up in their best clothes and walk the nine miles together to attend church. It was a day away from the fields, and J.C. and his family enjoyed it immensely.

When he was not in school or working, J.C. would fish, hunt, and run barefoot through the fields around the farm with his siblings. Running made him happy. He later

This is a recreation of a sharecropper's house at the Jesse Owens Memorial Park and Museum in Danville, Alabama. Young J.C. grew up sharecropping in Alabama, although he was often sick as a child.

said, "I always loved running. I wasn't very good at it, but I loved it because it was something you could do all by yourself, all under your own power. You could go in any direction, fast or slow as you wanted. . . . "[4] J.C.'s father was a talented runner who also enjoyed the activity when he had the chance, which was not often due to his heavy workload.

The direction J.C.'s parents always hoped they could head in was any direction that would lead them away from the backbreaking life of sharecropping. J.C.'s mother longed for a better life for her children and often suggested that the family should move from the farm. But Henry Owens was the grandson of a slave and had heard stories of what had happened to his family and other blacks when they had tried to defy the wishes of white men and branch out on their own. All his life, he avoided making eye contact with white men.[5]

Henry Owens, in fact, was even afraid to touch a book. His son later wrote, "He believed that if he laid a finger on one, someone in the family would fall suddenly ill, possibly die. . . . His parents and their parents had never been allowed to own a book, to say nothing of learning to read one. Slaves had been beaten to death for having books hidden in their homes."[6] This was done to keep them from educating

> "Slaves had been beaten to death for having books hidden in their homes."

themselves and at the mercy of their masters. Slave owners often feared educated slaves, because they might try to rise up against the institution of slavery. So even though slavery had been abolished decades earlier, the fear of the unknown kept Henry Owens saddled to another man's farm. It took a move by one of his children, and more of the constant urging from his wife, to get him off it.

During World War I, J.C.'s older sister Lillie had married and moved off the farm. She traveled north to Cleveland, Ohio, to look for a better life than Oakville had to offer. Shortly after she arrived in Cleveland, Lillie began writing letters to her family. The letters told of the many work opportunities Cleveland had to offer. In the big city, she wrote, blacks could find decent jobs in factories, feed their families, and live in better homes. Black children in Cleveland could receive better educations.

The daughter told her parents they should pack up their belongings and join her in Cleveland. With each letter she received, Emma Owens put more pressure on her husband to move. But farming was all Henry Owens knew. He knew nothing of Cleveland or of its many mills and factories. But the fearful Henry Owens finally gave in to his family's wishes. In the early 1920s, the Owens family sold most of their belongings, including their mules and farm equipment, packed up what few possessions they had left, and took a train north, leaving all they had ever known behind.

Great Migration

The Owens family was not the only black family to move north during this period in history. Between the late 1910s and early 1930s, roughly 1.5 million blacks left the South in search of better lives and jobs the North was rumored to offer. The period of history was called the Great Migration. Large numbers of blacks moved to northern cities, such as Chicago, New York, Cleveland, and Detroit.

For Henry Owens, life in Cleveland was not as perfect as he had been told it would be. But overall, it was a lot better than the farm had been. The Owens family moved into a rundown apartment on Cleveland's East Side—the poorer section of the city and an area occupied mostly by Polish immigrants.

The family found work almost immediately. The oldest Owens boys worked in a steel mill. Emma Owens and her daughters found cleaning jobs wherever they could. But work was difficult to come by for Henry Owens. In his mid-forties and worn down from a difficult life of sharecropping, he was not physically fit enough to keep up with the fast-paced work environment of a mill or factory. He worked whatever part-time jobs he could find. J.C. later wrote, "My father simply couldn't get steady work. He tried hard, but he didn't have a skill to his name except

This was the Owens family home in Cleveland.

for planting cotton. . . . The white man still controlled my father, only this time it was many white men—the people who didn't have a job for him."[7]

In his autobiography, Owens talked more about what life was like for his family in Cleveland. He wrote, "there were weeks when we came close to starving. Beans and onions. Potatoes and onions. Bread and onions. And never enough of them. . . . [My father] used to sit alone in the corner of the room where most of us slept and just stare at the mottled wall."[8]

Though he was only nine years old, J.C. also found work in Cleveland. He worked odd jobs each day after school. Those jobs included working in a shoe shop, delivering groceries, and loading freight cars. J.C.'s days were spent at Bolton Elementary School, which offered him a much better education than what he had received at his school in Alabama. The school's student body was more diverse than it had been in Alabama.

Bolton Elementary School presented the shy Alabama farm boy with several challenges. Adjusting to a big-city school was not easy. The education he had received in Alabama had left him behind other students of the same age. He was initially placed in first grade, where he was much bigger and older than the rest of his classmates. Even though he was soon advanced to second grade, J.C. still dwarfed his younger classmates.

Another adjustment J.C. had to make in the big city was overcoming his shyness. In one instance, that shyness changed the boy's life forever. When a teacher asked him his name, J.C. mumbled it to her in his Southern accent. The teacher did not hear him correctly, and wrote his name down as "Jesse." The shy boy was afraid to speak up and correct his teacher. He just agreed with what she wrote. The incorrect name stuck. From that moment on, Henry and Emma Owens's youngest son would forever be known as Jesse.

In this photo, an elementary classroom is shown in Cleveland in 1915.
Owens had to adjust to his new school in Cleveland, Bolton Elementary.

When Jesse enrolled at Fairmount Junior High School,
he met two people who would change his life dramatically.
The first was a thirteen-year-old girl named Minnie Ruth
Solomon. Jesse, now fifteen, was immediately attracted to
the gorgeous girl, who went by her middle name of Ruth.
The pair had a lot in common. Jesse said, "Like myself,
she had been born in the South and her parents had come
up from Georgia in the hopes of finding a better life."[9]
The two teens were inseparable, and Jesse soon discovered

Ruth's family also had moved with her parents from the South to Cleveland. Like Jesse's family, they had been part of what was called the Great Migration. Jesse said, "I fell in love with her from the first time we ever talked, and a little bit more every time after that until I thought I couldn't love her more than I did."[10] When that happened, Jesse asked Ruth to marry him. Both teens knew they were too young to legally do so. Ruth said yes anyway.

The second person Jesse met in junior high who helped change his life was a fifty-year-old physical education teacher named Charles Riley, who was the school's track and field coach. A skinny Irishman from Pennsylvania, Riley was physically almost the exact opposite of Jesse. But he knew talent when he spotted it, and he was always on the lookout for it. He had scouted Jesse for some time. He had observed the skinny kid horsing around on the playground and had noticed his athletic abilities. One day, Riley decided to approach this gifted youngster. Jesse said, "I'd noticed him watching me for a year or so, especially when we'd play games where there was running or jumping."[11]

What Riley noticed most was Jesse's potential. The coach also knew Jesse needed help to reach it. He asked Jesse if he wanted to join the school's track team. Jesse, beginning in his days on the farm in Oakville, always had loved to run. He was excited at Riley's offer—so excited, in fact, that when Riley told him he would have to come to practice to train every day after school, he agreed to do so.

The problem was, he had forgotten one important thing: He was not available to train after school. He had to work to help support his family. As soon as he remembered, the disappointed boy told his coach the news. He would not be able to join the team after all. For a kid with Jesse's potential, Riley was willing to compromise. He set up a training schedule that allowed Jesse to train before school.

Running gave Jesse an identity. Instead of being known as Jesse Owens, a poor black child living in Cleveland's ghetto, he became known as Jesse Owens, the runner. He began thinking about the activity day and night. Jesse said, "Every morning I got up an hour early, did my house chores, and hurried to school. The first few days I was afraid that Mr. Riley wouldn't show up. But he was always there at the end of the field, his big old watch dangling from a rope in his hand."[12] Riley knew talent when he saw it. He also knew that Jesse was raw and, with some training, could become a special runner.

> "But he was always there at the end of the field, his big old watch dangling from a rope in his hand."

Jesse also began to think of Riley as more than just a track coach. He began to think of him as a second father, referring to him as "Pop" rather than Mr. Riley, Coach Riley, or any of the other titles he could have used. This was a big step for Jesse, who, like his father, had never had

Charles Riley observes Jesse's running style. Riley became a mentor and father figure to Jesse in addition to helping him train.

a close relationship with a white man. It also was a big step for Riley. Racial segregation, keeping blacks separate from whites, still was very much a part of American society. It was a big step for a white man, such as Riley, to welcome a black child into his home. But Riley still welcomed Jesse with open arms. The coach's family did, as well. Riley's daughter said Jesse was "just a part of the family."[13] Jesse's family was also fine with the relationship. His mother was just happy that her son was being treated well, while his

◆◆◆◆◆◆◆◆◆◆◆◆◆◆◆◆◆◆◆◆◆◆◆◆◆◆

Charles Riley

Charles Riley certainly could relate to the hard work Jesse Owens had to do every day. Born in 1878, in Mauch Chunk, Pennsylvania, Riley had dropped out of high school to work as a miner and a mill worker. He eventually went back to school and attended Temple University in Philadelphia. Riley ended up as a teacher and coach at Fairmount Junior High School in Cleveland. He made so little money at the job that he had to manage a playground during the summer to help support his family.[14] Riley had three daughters and two sons, one who was disabled. Shortly after meeting the talented youngster, Riley unofficially made Jesse his sixth child, taking him under his wing and pushing him to greatness on and off the track.

father was often too self-obsessed to notice that his son was not home much.[15]

Jesse listened to everything his new coach told him, both on and off the track. He gained stamina. He gained strength in his legs. He followed all of Riley's training advice, even when it may have seemed somewhat strange, such as the day Riley took Jesse to a racetrack to watch and observe horses. Jesse had no idea how visiting a racetrack would improve his running, but Riley had a plan. He told Jesse to mimic the horses' running style: Focus on the finish line and make no other movements that do not help get you there. Another Riley technique was for Jesse to try to run as if the track were on fire, never letting his feet touch the ground for very long. This kept his legs pumping as quickly as possible and helped propel him down the track. Jesse adopted both those suggestions and used them his entire life.

Riley also helped Jesse train his mind. He constantly told Jesse, "Train for four years from next Friday." It was Riley's way of getting Jesse to focus on long-term goals and not worry about what might happen tomorrow.

Jesse trained hard every day—his only goals were to please his coach and improve as an athlete. But the mentor had loftier goals for his subject. He knew there was greatness inside his star pupil. He planned to work Jesse as hard as possible to get that potential to come out. Jesse had no idea what Riley had planned for him. Jesse just loved to run.

Chapter 3

Breaking
Records

Jesse's exceptional running and jumping abilities translated well into the sport of track and field. His speed made him a natural for the sprints, or shorter races, and his leaping ability made him a natural for the broad jump, an event known today as the long jump. Jesse's hard work with Riley began to pay off in ways that were measurable. When Coach Charles Riley finally began timing Jesse in his runs, he discovered that his sprint times were excellent. In fact, they were so good that even Riley had a hard time believing them.

One day, Jesse competed in an informal 100-yard race against other boys his age. As the boys began running down a Cleveland street, Riley started his stopwatch. When they had completed the distance, 100 yards, with Jesse in first place, Riley looked down at his stopwatch.

He could not believe what it said. Jesse had clocked in at eleven seconds. At the time, the 100-yard (approximately 91 meters) world record was just under ten seconds. Jesse was a little more than one second away from being the fastest runner in the world. And he was still in junior high school. How far could this boy actually go?

In 1928, Jesse began to compete in official school track meets. The meets would give Riley a better measure of how good Jesse really was. He quickly found out. In his first year of track, Jesse set junior high school world records in both the high jump and the long jump, in which he leapt just short of 23 feet. The adult world record in that event at the time was a little less than 26 feet. Jesse also dominated all the running events he entered.

Riley now believed Jesse had enough natural talent to become an Olympic champion. But first, the boy would need to see what it took to become one. What better way to do that than to meet an Olympic champion? Riley arranged for Charlie Paddock to speak at Jesse's school. At the time, Paddock was one of the world's fastest men. He had won Olympic medals in both 1920 and 1924. Over the years, he had broken several records, and he had tied the 100-meter world record in 1921. After Paddock's speech, Riley introduced Jesse to the Olympic champion. Jesse was inspired and in awe. After the meeting, Jesse set his sights on the loftiest of goals: He wanted to be an Olympic champion, too.

When Jesse began competing in track meets, he set junior high world records in the long jump and high jump. This is the 1928 Fairmount Junior High championship track team.

◆ ◆ ◆ ◆ ◆

In 1930, Jesse entered East Technical High School in Cleveland, an integrated school more focused on teaching its students a trade rather than showing them how to read and write. The move to high school meant Jesse, now seventeen years old, would have to leave his coach and father figure behind. Coach Riley had taken Jesse to great heights in junior high school, but East Tech had its own coach, Edgar Weil. Weil's background was in football,

Charlie Paddock

Jesse Owens was not the only person to idolize Charlie Paddock when he met him. The larger-than-life Paddock had a big impact on most everyone he came across, not only because of his outstanding running credentials but also because of his outgoing personality and the exciting stories he had to share. Born in 1900, in Gainesville, Texas, Paddock served in the military and competed in the Inter-Allied Games in 1919. His success there was a stepping-stone to the 1920 Olympics in Antwerp, Belgium. There, he won the 100 meters and was part of the gold medal 4x100-meter relay team. He also took second place in the 200-meter run. Four years later, at the Olympic Games in Paris, Paddock finished second in the 200 meters. He competed in the 1928 Olympics in Amsterdam, Netherlands, but failed to qualify for the 200-meter finals. On the track, Paddock's finishing style gathered a lot of attention. At the end of each race, he would leap toward the finish tape. His Olympic success launched him into a career in journalism and acting. He starred in such films as *The Olympic Hero, High School Hero*, and *The Campus Flirt*. In 1943, Paddock died in a plane crash near Sitka, Alaska, while serving in the military. In 1981, Paddock was portrayed in *Chariots of Fire*, a film about the 1924 Olympics.

a sport that Jesse had tried but had given up because it took too much time away from running. Weil understood that he was no expert on track and field. He also knew Jesse was a special athlete and needed more help than the coaching he could give. So Weil asked Riley to be his assistant coach. It turned out to be a great move.

Under Riley's control, Jesse continued to thrive as an athlete and grow as a person. On the track, he continued in high school where he had left off in junior high. He easily won most of the events he entered. By 1932, Jesse had earned a reputation as a tough and talented competitor. He was so good, in fact, that competing in the Olympics was no longer just a childhood dream. There was a good chance it could become a reality. Everyone in the city of Cleveland knew it. At one meet there on June 11, 1932, the eighteen-year-old Owens ran the 100 meters in 10.3 seconds. That time broke the current world record, which was held by Charlie Paddock. But the record was not allowed to stand because it was ruled that there was too much wind at Owens's back during the race. Record or not, it was a remarkable feat. It now looked like Owens could make it to the Olympics.

The United States was scheduled to host that year's Olympics, and Los Angeles was to be the host city. To be able to compete in the Olympics, an athlete had to race in one of several Olympic qualifying meets. If he made it, then he would advance to the Olympic trials. Owens's qualifying meet was held later in June at Northwestern

Charlie Paddock wins a race in Santa Barbara, California, in 1922, and displays his famous finishing style of leaping toward the finish line.

University in Evanston, Illinois. It was the first time that Owens had ever faced world-class competition.

Eddie Tolan, a star African-American athlete, who went on to win gold medals in the 100 and 200 meters in Los Angeles, was in the field. Owens entered three events: the 100 meters, the 200 meters, and the long jump. He was outclassed in all three and did not qualify for the Olympic trials. Owens was devastated and embarrassed by his losses.

After the meet, Owens told one reporter, "I haven't got the heart to see Mr. Riley. He must be terribly ashamed of me. I don't know what was the matter. I ran as fast as I could . . . but I just didn't have it."[1] Owens even felt as if he had let the newspaper reporter, who had been covering him all season, down. He said, "It was nice for you to try and make me feel good, but I'll bet you're as much ashamed of me as anybody else."[2]

In truth, no one was ashamed of Owens, except for himself. The athletes he was competing against were older, more powerful, and more experienced. Track and field athletes generally do not reach their peak until they are in their twenties. At the time of the meet in Evanston, Owens was only eighteen. He still had a bright future ahead of him.

> "I ran as fast as I could . . . but I just didn't have it."

It is also likely that Owens's mind had been focused on his personal life on the day of the competition. Several significant events had happened to Owens around the time of the meet. His father recently had been hit by a car while crossing a street. Henry Owens's leg was broken, leaving him unable to work to contribute income for his family. Jesse felt pressure to drop out of school, quit running, and help his family by working more than he already did. All his older brothers had quit school to do just that. As each one of those brothers married, they even moved their new spouses into the Owens family home so they could afford to live. Sometimes there would be more than a dozen people living in the home. But the Owens parents kept encouraging their youngest son to continue running. Despite his parents's well wishes, that was not easy for Jesse to do. He cared deeply about his family but decided to bow to their wishes. And they insisted he stay in school.

Another issue weighing heavily on Jesse's mind at this time was his longtime relationship with Ruth Solomon. When Owens was competing in the Evanston meet, the sixteen-year-old Ruth was eight months pregnant with his child. On August 8, 1932, that child, Gloria Shirley Owens, was born. To support her, Ruth dropped out of school to get a job and lived at home with her parents, who had banned Jesse from their house. Despite all the chaos in her life, Ruth continued to support Jesse's running, just as his parents had.

Whether or not Ruth and Jesse Owens were married when their first daughter was born has been a source of debate for decades. Owens said that the two had driven to Erie, Pennsylvania, and gotten married in 1932. But historians have not found a marriage certificate to back up Owens's claims and generally believe the couple's wedding to have taken place in 1935.

Now a new father, Owens returned to East Technical High School for his senior year. As one might imagine, he was massively popular with his fellow students, even though most of them were white. He was so popular, in

Great Depression

Poor as she was, Ruth Owens deserves a lot of credit for allowing Jesse to continue running rather than asking him to drop out of school and get a full-time job to help support their daughter. Her blessing was especially impressive, because at the time her baby was born, the United States was in the midst of the Great Depression. The Depression began in the late 1920s, as the economy struggled due to a decline in agriculture and bank failures and worsened when investors lost billions of dollars in the stock market crash of 1929. In the following years, millions of people lost their jobs, their homes, and all their savings. Stores closed, people starved, and food riots sprung up across the United States. It was the worst economic crisis in the history of the country. Because the U.S. economy is so powerful, other countries also felt the impact of the Great Depression. And Europe was still trying to recover from World War I. The Depression ended as World War II approached, in 1939, as countries began to increase their production of war materials and put a lot of people to work making them.

fact, that he was voted student body president. By now, his reputation as a star athlete was also quite large. Several major colleges began to recruit him to come and compete for their track teams. Owens wrote, " . . . offers started to come in. Some days there were three or four different letters in the mail. A lot of the universities sent someone all the way to Cleveland to meet me face to face."[3]

Making the decision to go to college was not easy for Owens. He knew his parents counted on him to help support them, although they had given him their blessing to continue running. Now, he had a child and a girlfriend he needed to support, too. How would he be able to do all those things, pay for college, *and* continue running? It seemed impossible. Owens was overwhelmed. He knew what he had to do. He would have to say good-bye to running. Owens said, "So I went to coach Charles Riley one morning, chokingly thanked him for everything he had done—and he had done just about everything at times—and told him I wouldn't be back."[4]

Coach Riley was not about to see his star pupil give up now. He had spent too many early mornings training him before school. They had worked too hard, and Owens had too much potential to just give up. So Riley drove 150 miles south to Columbus, Ohio, to meet with Larry Snyder, the head track and field coach at Ohio State University. Ohio State had been one of the universities that really wanted Owens on its team. Ohio State had a highly successful track and field program. Adding a

Jesse Owens crosses the finish line during a race in a high school track meet. Jesse's success in high school attracted a lot of attention from college recruiters.

potential superstar athlete like Owens would make it even more successful.

Riley told Snyder about Owens's situation. He told him all about Owens having to give up on school so he could work to support his family. Riley also said Owens was willing to work while he attended school to pay for his tuition and earn some money to send home to help support his family. Today, Owens would not have to worry about paying for his tuition, because schools can award scholarships to athletes. But in 1933, colleges were not allowed to offer any athletic scholarships. Athletes had to pay their own way through school. If Owens came to Ohio State, Snyder said, he could help the young athlete get a job.

Riley could not wait to return to Cleveland to tell Owens the news. He could take care of his many personal responsibilities and still go to college. When Owens heard the news, he was ecstatic. He later wrote, "I was five inches taller than he was, but I threw my arms around Coach Riley and kissed him."[5]

> "I was five inches taller than he was, but I threw my arms around Coach Riley and kissed him."

Before Owens could focus on what his life at Ohio State would be like, he had one final high school track meet to worry about: the National Interscholastic Championships.

There, on June 17, 1933, at Stagg Field in Chicago, Owens ran 9.4 seconds in the 100-yard dash, tying the world record held by American Frank Wykoff. Owens also set high school records in the 220-yard dash and long jump.[6]

Owens's achievement in Chicago was spectacular. When he returned to Cleveland, the city held a parade in his honor. He and his parents rode through the town in the backseat of a convertible, waving to the large crowd that had gathered alongside the road to witness the event. Coach Riley was in a car right behind them. For everyone involved in the life of Jesse Owens, it was a moment of celebration. He finished his high school career having run seventy-nine races, losing only four times. But no one knew how he would fare in college. For the first time ever, he would be living miles away from his family and miles away from his surrogate father, the man he called Pop.

Chapter 4

Greatest Day in History

esse Owens arrived on the Ohio State University campus in the fall of 1933, a wide-eyed twenty-year-old away from home for the first time in his life. In his hometown, he was a star. In Columbus, he was one of thousands of young adults looking to discover who he was and learning about what the world had to offer him. Owens quickly discovered the college world had both bad and good to offer him and that there were some things being a star athlete could not help him conquer.

One of those things was the racism that still existed in much of the United States. When Owens entered Ohio State University, the school had only one men's dormitory, and Owens was not allowed to live there because he was black. He had to live in a nearby boardinghouse

When he traveled with the track team, Owens and the team's other black athletes often had to stay in "black-only" hotels.

with several other black students. He and his housemates were not allowed to go into most movie theaters in Columbus. Restaurants near the campus would not serve black students. They had to cook their own meals or eat in the student cafeteria. When he traveled with the track team, Owens and the team's other black athletes often had to stay in "black-only" hotels.

Though it was only 150 miles away from Cleveland, the Columbus school was a world away when it came to racial tolerance. According to one Owens biographer, "Ohio State had a notoriously bad reputation for racially prejudicial attitudes and policies."[1] Some members of the black media even criticized Owens for choosing to attend Ohio State because of this.

Years later, Owens wrote about one particularly negative experience he had traveling on his way to a track meet. He recalled stopping by a roadside diner in southern Indiana and watching his white teammates go inside to get breakfast while he and the other black athletes waited in the car for the food their teammates would bring them. When it arrived, Owens wrote, a big man from inside the diner was not far behind. The man shouted,

"I don't want money to feed no *niggers*!" and reached inside the window to grab the plates of food, spilling them all over the place.[2] Owens wrote, "It had happened a hundred times, maybe a thousand. I lost count long ago."[3]

Owens worked in the school student cafeteria at Ohio State and received free meals for doing so. He also had two other jobs: working in the library and operating a freight elevator at night. Both the latter jobs allowed him to study while he worked. The extra study time was important, especially for a student who often struggled with his grades. But even with the additional time, Owens did not do well academically. By the time spring rolled around, he had been put on academic probation because of his low grades. Owens struggled with his grades the entire time he attended the university. Being away from his family in Cleveland was not easy. Add three jobs on top of that and even the most-talented student would have a hard time succeeding. Owens never had been the most-talented student, though he always studied hard. It was the same work ethic his father had instilled in him back on the Alabama farm. The same one he had used to become such a successful athlete in high school. In college, that work ethic would help him become an even better athlete. His new coach, Larry Snyder, had a lot to do with that.

A former pilot instructor in World War I, Snyder picked up where Charles Riley had left off. He pushed Owens hard and taught him new techniques he felt would make the athlete better at each of the disciplines

Jesse Owens training with Coach Larry Snyder
at Ohio State University in 1935.

he competed in. For the sprints, that meant refining the way Owens started each race to give him more of an early boost. He also helped him in other ways. Owens said, "He helped me to make all of my movement lean forward—the mark of a good runner. He taught me little ways to stop bobbing when I ran, and how not to strain."[4]

In the long jump, Snyder pointed out to Owens that one of his legs was stronger than the other. If he wanted to jump farther, the coach said, Owens would need to develop more power in his weaker leg. Owens worked hard on that as well as on improving his jumping form. Owens said, "Larry was a real expert at that event and spent a lot of hours showing me the correct form."[5]

Snyder was well known in the world of track and field as an innovator. He would try new training techniques to help his athletes get better. One he was best known for was having his athletes train to the sounds of music playing on a record player. He felt it would help the athletes relax and that they would benefit from the rhythms of the songs.[6] Today, many athletes would find it strange to not have music playing when they worked out.

Owens was not allowed to compete in college during his freshman year at Ohio State. That decision had nothing to do with his problems in the classroom. It was simply because the rules stated that freshmen were not allowed to compete at any college. So Owens could not participate in any varsity track meets. But he could, and did, practice. And he competed in several amateur events. In the spring

Larry Snyder

Jesse Owens was not the only athlete to benefit greatly from Larry Snyder's innovative coaching techniques. During his career at Ohio State University, Snyder's athletes won eight Olympic gold medals and set fourteen world records. Part of Snyder's success came because he had been an athlete and could relate to many of the issues his athletes had to deal with. Before coming to Ohio State University to coach the track team, Snyder had been a star hurdler at the school. In 1960, Snyder was named head coach of the U.S. Olympic track team. In 1978, he was inducted into the U.S.A. Track & Field Hall of Fame. Snyder, born in 1896 in Canton, Ohio, died in 1982.

of 1934, Owens ended the outdoor track season at the Amateur Athletic Union (AAU) national championships in New York City. There, he finished second in the 100 meters to Ralph Metcalfe, who had won the silver medal in the event in the 1932 Olympics in Los Angeles.

Owens was well known around the country, in and outside track circles, before he even had been eligible to compete for Ohio State University's varsity team. But once his sophomore year came around and he became varsity eligible, Owens's fame—and marks—really took off. On one day in particular, Saturday, May 25, 1935, Owens set

Ralph Metcalfe (right) defeats Jesse Owens (left) in an
AAU track meet on June 30, 1934. Only a couple months earlier,
Metcalfe had defeated Owens at the AAU national championships.

a standard so high some have called it "the greatest single
day in the history of man's athletic achievements."[7]

Owens's great feat came at the Big Ten Championship
meet at Ferry Field in Ann Arbor, Michigan. In the span
of seventy minutes, Owens set three world records and
tied a fourth. The records included the 220-yard dash, the

220-yard hurdles, and the long jump. He tied the world record in the 100-yard dash.

Owens's long jump of 26 feet, 8¼ inches was not surpassed for an astonishing twenty-five years. He had achieved it in a dramatic fashion. Before his jump, Owens had placed a white handkerchief next to the old record to show him what he needed to do. Looking on from the stands as Owens achieved greatness: his first coach, Charles Riley, who had driven down from Cleveland to see the meet.

> There was no pain, so Owens continued his amazing march toward the record books.

Owens's feat was made more remarkable by the fact that he almost did not compete in the meet. Days earlier, he had injured his back falling down some stairs at school. On the day of the meet, Owens still was in severe pain. Coach Snyder told his star athlete he was not going to allow him to compete. Snyder was afraid Owens would suffer a serious injury, shattering his Olympic dreams and ruining his entire career. But that is when Owens's competitive fire came out. He went through his regular warm-ups and talked his coach into letting him try the 100-yard dash. If he felt any pain, he said, he would drop out. There was no pain, so Owens continued his amazing march toward the record books.

Later that year, Owens went on to win college national championships in four events: the 100-yard dash, the

Jesse Owens crosses the finish line during the 220-yard dash at
the Big Ten Championship on May 25, 1935. On this historic day,
Owens broke three world records and tied another one.

◆◆◆◆◆◆◆◆◆◆◆◆◆◆◆◆◆◆◆◆◆◆◆◆◆◆◆

Jesse Owens's Nicknames

Jesse Owens had many nicknames throughout his life. His first nickname, "Jesse," was of course given to him by a schoolteacher who thought that was his real name. As he grew and began to excel at running, Owens gained other nicknames. Some of those that were considered acceptable at the time they were given to him would be considered racist today and are no longer used. These include, "The Scarlet Comet," "The Midnight Express," "The Dark Streak," and "The Ebony Antelope."[8] Others, such as "The Buckeye Bullet," have stuck and are still used in reference to Owens today.

220-yard dash, the low hurdles, and the long jump. During that meet, he scored forty of Ohio State's forty-one points. Despite Owens's domination, Ohio State never won a national title in track and field when Owens was there.

Owens's fame shot through the roof after his achievements at the conference meet and national championships. In his autobiography, Owens wrote: "After that, just about everything I did seemed to get in the newspapers. The sickly poverty case from Oakville had become a famous athlete."[9] Unfortunately for Owens, he was about to experience several of the negative effects fame can have on a person.

—◦◦◦—

One happened that June in Los Angeles. Owens was in town to compete in a track meet. It was his first time on the West Coast and, like most tourists would, Owens decided to take in some of the sights the big city had to offer. He met several celebrities there, including Clark Gable, Mae West, Will Rogers, and Mickey Rooney. That was not the problem. The problem was who he was with when he was doing all these activities. Her name was Quincella Nickerson, and she was the daughter of a wealthy California businessman.

Because Owens was such a star, photographers were snapping pictures of the couple during their outings. Some of those photographs ended up in newspapers across the country, including one in Cleveland seen by Ruth Solomon, the mother of Owens's child and the supposed love of his life. She was furious, especially because some of those newspapers reported that Nickerson and Owens were engaged. Owens immediately began his damage control. He explained the situation to one reporter: "We were at a party and Miss Nickerson asked to see my fraternity pin. I took it off and handed it to her, then stepped into another room for a minute. When I came back she was wearing it. Just before I left the West Coast I asked her for it. She cried a little but handed it over. I got out as fast as I could."[10]

That explanation was not enough of an apology for Solomon. She threatened to sue Owens for not honoring his promise to marry her, which was a regular practice

Jesse Owens with Minnie Ruth Solomon on their wedding day.

for scorned women of the day.[11] Owens quickly fixed the problem, traveling back to Cleveland on July 5. That day, he married Solomon in a hastily planned wedding ceremony. One magazine story reported the day in detail. The story read, "Owens hurried to a preacher, married a Cleveland beauty-parlor maid named Minnie Ruth Solomon, entrained for Buffalo alone after promising to bring her a ring when he returned."[12] It was not exactly romantic, but it did help cure what had been a major public relations headache for Owens. It was not the only one Owens would have to deal with in his lifetime.

The personal nightmare also affected Owens on the track. The day before his official marriage to Ruth—which also all but confirmed the two had not married earlier, as Owens said they had—Owens fared poorly at the Amateur Athletic Union's national championship meet in Lincoln, Nebraska. He lost every event he entered that day. He lost the 100 meters, finishing third behind Eulace Peacock of Temple University and Ralph Metcalfe, who also beat Owens in the 200 meters. Peacock also won the long jump, with Owens finishing a close second. One reporter called Peacock's wins over Owens "one of the greatest double upsets in the history of track."[13] Because Owens was fresh off his phenomenal achievement at the Big Ten Championships, the reporter was not far off the mark with his comments. Peacock and Owens—both Alabama-born black men whose families had battled racism for decades—squared off several times in 1935, and Peacock won most of those duels. Despite this, the two men maintained a cordial relationship.

A worn-out Owens returned to Cleveland to finish out his summer break and get some much-needed rest. He lived with his daughter and his wife in her family's home. He took a job pumping gas at a service station owned by Alonzo Wright. Owens also had worked there the previous two summers. Taking a break from competition seemed to be what Owens needed to do. His body and mind

Jesse Owens working as a gas station attendant during the summer of 1935.
He worked the summer job to help support his family.

were very tired. In just a few weeks, he had gone from an unbeatable star to one who was capable of being beaten in any race. Unfortunately for Owens, another controversy was right around the corner.

In August, the Amateur Athletic Union questioned whether Owens was eligible to compete as an amateur. At issue was some $159 Owens had been paid by the Ohio state legislature for work he had done as an honorary page. The legislature did not meet in the summer, but still paid Owens, which raised eyebrows with the AAU. The athletic union believed Owens was being paid for work he did not do, which would be considered an illegal athletic scholarship. If that was the case, the AAU had the power to declare Owens ineligible to compete in amateur events, including the Olympics. He would be considered a professional athlete. For years, Owens had focused on making it to the Olympics. Declaring him a professional would have been devastating. At the end of August, the AAU ruled in Owens's favor. He had to pay back the $159, but he did not lose his amateur eligibility. Owens's Olympic dream was still alive. But he was not there yet. There were plenty more hurdles to clear first.

Chapter 5

Defusing the Dictator

O wens was a well-known athlete by the time he entered his junior year at Ohio State University. He was also well known as a poor student. In fact, he was suspended from the track team for part of the year due to his bad grades and had to train on his own. He worked hard on both his grades and his athletic training and was allowed to rejoin the track team in the spring.

On the track, the well-rested Owens picked up where he had left off the previous season, winning meets and setting records. On May 16, 1936, in Wisconsin, Owens broke the world record in the 100-yard dash with a time of 9.3 seconds. In June, he won the 100-yard dash, 220-yard dash, 200-meter hurdles, and long jump at the collegiate national championship meet. It was the same four events he had won at the meet the previous season, giving him a record-setting eight in total.

Owens's most-important accomplishment of the year, to that point at least, came July 11 and 12 at the U.S. Olympic Trials on New York City's Randall's Island. With his top rival, Eulace Peacock, out with an injury, Owens easily won the 100 meters, with Ralph Metcalfe second and Frank Wykoff third. Then Owens capped his first day of competition with an easy win in the long jump. The next day, he made it a trifecta, dominating the 200 meters in twenty-one seconds flat. Owens was heading to the Olympics in three events. His longtime dream was realized. Now it was time to set a new goal: become an Olympic champion.

Owens and the dozens of other Americans who had qualified at the meet were fortunate to even be going to the Olympics at all. Four years earlier, the International Olympic Committee had awarded the 1936 Olympic Games to Germany rather than to Spain. The move seemed relatively harmless at the time. But, in 1933, the Nazi Party gained control of Germany, and the situation began to change rapidly. The party's leader was a man named Adolf Hitler, who believed the "Aryan" race—pure-blooded Germans who were often tall with blond hair and blue eyes—was superior to every other type of people on the planet. Those he called "sub-human" included Jews, people with disabilities, homosexuals, blacks, and many other groups of people. Hitler's goal was to eliminate all non-Aryans from Germany. Hitler viewed Jews as his primary "racial" enemy. Hitler and the Nazi Party developed harsh policies toward Jews. He took away most of their freedoms, imprisoned them in concentration camps, and sometimes killed them. During Hitler's reign, tens of thousands of Jews fled Germany to avoid being discriminated against.

> Others argued that the United States was basically doing the same thing to its African Americans as Germany was to its Jews.

Many in the United States and other nations believed their countries should boycott the 1936 Olympics as a way of protesting Hitler's treatment of Jews and other non-Aryans. Others argued that the United States was basically doing the same thing to its African Americans as Germany was to its Jews. On some levels, those people had a point. Racism still existed in the United States, just as it did in Germany. In 1935, there had been eighteen documented lynchings, or illegal executions often done by hanging, of black people in the southern United States.[1]

For a long while, it seemed as if a boycott of the Olympics might occur. However, near the end of 1935, the American Olympic Association and the Amateur Athletic Union decided it would be okay to send their athletes to Germany to compete in both the Winter and Summer Olympics. This, of course, was welcome news for

Adolf Hitler

Today, Adolf Hitler is generally remembered as one of the most brutal leaders in the history of the world, even by people in Germany, the country he ruled from 1933 to 1945 as leader of the Nazi Party. But people did not always feel that way about Hitler. When he came into power in 1933, Germany was a weak country, still reeling from its defeat in World War I and affected by the Great Depression. When he became leader, Hitler helped restore the economy and rebuild Germany's military. He also acted on his hatred of Jews, relegating them to second-class citizens and placing restrictions on where they could work, where they could live, and even who they could marry. Many Jews were harmed and placed in prisons called concentration camps. In 1939, Hitler led Germany in an invasion of Poland. It was the beginning of World War II. Germany's army conquered several other countries. Eventually, they lost the war but not before killing approximately 6 million Jews in what became known as the Holocaust. When enemy forces approached the Berlin bunker in which Hitler was living in 1945, Hitler committed suicide. He was fifty-six years old.

the twenty-two-year-old Owens and the rest of the athletes who had trained most of their lives for the opportunity to compete at the Olympics. The Olympics only come once every four years. Those who missed that opportunity for whatever reason often never again had the chance to make it there.

On the morning of July 15, 1936, the United States Olympic team boarded a luxurious steamship, the SS *Manhattan*, in New York. The team was excited to begin making its way across the Atlantic Ocean. The departure itself was a large event, with some ten thousand people coming to wish the athletes good luck and good-bye. One newspaper account said, "It was probably the grandest and noisiest farewell New York ever knew. Ashore and afloat, and even in the air—where airplanes and blimps soared and dipped—exuberance was so manifest it almost knocked your hat off. It was a virtual tornado of massed joy because the team was off to the games. . . ."[2]

More than one thousand people were on board, 334 of them athletes.[3] Even the ship's stacks were patriotic, painted in a bold red, white, and blue. A few dozen other American athletes were either already in Germany or were to arrive later. Most of the rest of the passengers departing from New York on July 15 were either involved with the Olympics in some fashion, such as officials or coaches, or spectators who would be attending the games.

Owens was one of eighteen black athletes on the American team. It was the largest number of blacks ever

Jesse Owens practices the long jump aboard the SS *Manhattan* while traveling to Berlin, Germany, for the Olympic Games.

sent to an Olympics and the largest U.S. team in history. As one might expect, life aboard the *Manhattan* during its weeklong journey across the Atlantic Ocean was festive. Owens and the rest of the ship's passengers dined on good food, danced, and partied. Owens and his fellow competitors trained as best they could aboard a seven-hundred-foot ship traveling across an ocean. Some were able to make it work; others were not. Some of the athletes put on so much weight during the voyage that it hampered their performances in the Olympics. Owens managed to avoid most of the things that might hurt his performance. He said he countered his " . . . boredom, homesickness and anxiety by sleeping, not by eating foolishly."[4]

The SS *Manhattan* arrived in Hamburg, Germany, on July 23. The next day, the athletes left the ship and boarded two trains for a three-hour ride to Berlin, the host city of the games. Huge crowds greeted them with cheers at every stop along the way—at the train station, town hall, and, finally, at the spectacular Olympic Village, where the athletes would be staying during the games. The village was located a few miles outside Berlin and featured all the amenities the athletes would need to continue training for the games. The setting was as relaxed as could be expected. At night, the athletes would even gather to sing songs together. Owens hung out with athletes from his own country as well as those from several other countries.

Years later, Owens wrote about his arrival in Germany. He said, "The greetings I received in the German capital had been bittersweet. There were cheering crowds for me when I got off the train. But then I saw newspapers which told of hated American 'black auxiliary tribes' of which I was supposed to be the leader."[5]

Nonetheless, Owens always seemed jovial while in Berlin, especially to the many German children who crowded around him when he was practicing at the Olympic Village, hoping to see and perhaps get an autograph from the world-record holder. As often as he could, Owens gave them what they were looking for. Owens was treated equally well on the rare occasions he ventured out of the Olympic Village and onto the streets of Germany. Everyone knew who he was. According to one of Owens's college and Olympic teammates, David Albritton, the men in one German bar even came up and asked the black athletes to dance with their wives.[6] If racism was rampant in Germany, Owens did not seem to be experiencing much of it firsthand.

> "The greetings I received in the German capital had been bittersweet."

The Summer Olympic Games officially began on Saturday, August 1, 1936. The world was watching them, and it was Hitler's chance to show the world that his country was not as bad as people had made it out to be.

Jesse Owens signs autographs for German
fans from atop the U.S. Olympic Team's bus
during the opening ceremony of the Olympic Games.

He ordered all the antisemitic (prejudice against Jews) signs to be taken down prior to the Olympics. He wanted his country to look its best and to give off an image that everything was going well.

Hitler had made many improvements to Germany, which was attempting to recover from its defeat nearly two decades earlier in World War I. Under Hitler's rule, there were more jobs, and Germany's economy grew strong. He oversaw the building of dozens of dams, railroads, and superhighways called autobahns, where there were no speed limits and people could drive their cars as fast as they wanted. At the same time, Germany's military was rapidly expanding. The European country was once again becoming a powerful nation. It also was on the verge of another war, though that was a few years away.

Germans had to pay a high price for the improvements Hitler and his party brought to their country. Aside from dealing with the persecution of Jews and other non-Aryans, they had to give up other freedoms many people across the world took for granted. The government controlled newspapers and other forms of media. Freedom of speech was virtually nonexistent, and those who spoke out against Hitler were punished. Hitler arrested all political opponents and put them in concentration camps. Speaking out against Hitler or publishing materials bashing him could put a person in such a camp, and many were killed.

A crowd of 110,000 in the Olympic Stadium watched the opening ceremony. Dressed in his brown military

This poster shows the *Hindenburg* flying over the
Olympic Stadium during the opening ceremony of
the Olympic Games. Adolf Hitler wanted
Germany's Olympics to be a dazzling spectacle.

◆◆◆◆◆◆◆◆◆◆◆◆◆◆◆◆◆◆◆◆◆◆◆◆

History of the Olympics

Exactly when the first Olympic Games were held is anyone's guess. Many historians believe the Games began in 776 B.C. in the city of Olympia in ancient Greece and were created to honor Zeus, the king of the Greek gods. People traveled from afar to see the very best athletes compete in such events as boxing, wrestling, running, and even events for trumpeters. The ancient Games were held every four years for nearly twelve hundred years.

The first modern Olympic Games were held in 1896 in Athens, Greece. Fourteen countries competed in the games. The first modern Olympic champion was American James Connolly, who won the triple jump. He received a silver medal and an olive branch for his victory. The modern Olympics continue to evolve with time. Today, the Olympics are broken into Winter and Summer Games, with each one being held every four years, so there is an Olympics every other year. Gold medals are now given to the winner of each event, with silver medals going to second-place finishers, and bronze medals to those who finish third.

uniform, Hitler watched from his viewing box as the athletes marched into the stadium. Some even offered him a Nazi salute, holding their right arm straight out and pointed slightly up. The Americans did not salute him at all.[7] The giant German airship *Hindenburg* hovered over the stadium. Inside the stadium, Nazi swastika symbols were everywhere. After some music, chants from the crowd, and the releasing of twenty thousand white doves—symbolizing peace—a blond-haired runner entered the stadium carrying a small torch and lit the stadium's big cauldron. The games were under way.

Competition began the following day. Owens easily passed through the preliminary heats of the 100 meters. The semifinals and finals were scheduled for the next day, August 3. Owens breezed into the finals, winning that race in 10.3 seconds. Ralph Metcalfe was second and Martinus Osendarp of the Netherlands third. Standing atop the podium during the medal ceremony, Owens shed tears as he received his first gold medal and the U.S. national anthem began to play. Owens later called it the happiest moment in his life.

Whether or not, as legend has it, he refused to shake Owens's hand, Hitler clearly was not happy seeing an American, especially a *black* American, win the most-celebrated Olympic event. He also was not happy to hear his fellow countrymen screaming Owens's name. One American who claimed to have seen Hitler's reaction said, " . . . it was so tense you could hardly breathe. Would it get violent? With him you never could tell. He certainly let us know he didn't approve of that black man having a gold medal."[8]

For his part, Owens simply pressed on. The next day was Tuesday, August 4, a busy one. First up was the first round of the long jump competition. Qualifying for the finals should have been easy for Owens, the world-record holder in the event. But it was not. On his first jump, Owens ran down the runway and straight into the pit. He thought it was just a warm-up, but warm-ups were not allowed at the Olympics. His first jump was a foul. Now he only had two jumps left. He appeared to have qualified on his second attempt, but the judge raised a red flag, signifying the jump would not be counted because Owens ran past the takeoff board before jumping. Another foul.

With one final chance to qualify, Owens was terrified. He did not want to fail. He wrote, "If I fouled again—if Jesse Owens, the world champion, lost out in the trials— I knew I'd be through. . . . So this next jump—if it turned out to be another bad one—could truly be my last."[9]

What Owens says happened next has been debated over the years. Some historians believe it did not occur and that Owens made it up. But in his

> "So this next jump—if it turned out to be another bad one— could truly be my last."

autobiography, Owens said Germany's star long jumper, the blond-haired, blue-eyed Luz Long, came to his aid. Owens wrote, "He wanted to *help* me. . . . He advised me to draw a line a whole foot in *back* of the takeoff board and jump from there. That way I *couldn't* foul."[10] Owens said he took his rival's advice and that it helped him easily qualify on his third leap. He even set a new Olympic record. Owens spent the rest of the afternoon breezing

Jesse Owens makes a big splash in the sand to set a new Olympic record during the long jump event at the 1936 Olympics.

through the 200-meter qualifying heats and advancing to the long jump finals. They were held that evening, and the battle for the gold medal came down to two jumpers: Owens and Long, his new German friend.

Their battle went back and forth. On his second jump, Long took the lead. On his second jump, Owens took it back. Long had one final shot to do the same. But as he bolted down the runway on his third attempt, Long overran the takeoff board. The judge's red flag went up in the air, giving the gold medal to Owens. It was his second of the Olympics. He could have stopped competing and began celebrating. But Owens decided to take his third jump anyway. Owens darted down the runway, leapt, then soared into the air with his arms waving and legs peddling. When Owens landed his momentum was so great that he fell forward on his hands in the sand and nearly stumbled out of the end of the pit. His mark: 26 feet, 5 5/16 inches. It was another Olympic record.

Long was the first to congratulate his rival and did so with a big hug. Competition had presented the two men an opportunity to form a friendship. They did, and that friendship would last a lifetime. Owens said, "It took a lot of courage for him to befriend me in front of Hitler. You can melt down all the medals and cups I have and they wouldn't be a plating on the 24-karat friendship I felt for Luz Long at that moment. Hitler must have gone crazy watching us embrace."[11]

Luz Long

In no event had the United States been more dominant than the long jump. In the entire history of the modern Olympic Games, only once had a non-American won gold in the event. In 1936, the Germans thought they had just the person to break America's dominance. His name was Carl Ludwig "Luz" Long. Long, a twenty-three-year-old student from Leipzig, was Adolf Hitler's picture of a perfect human—blond hair, blue eyes, and six feet tall. That fact made it even more painful for Hitler when Owens defeated Long.

Long and Owens formed a bond during their time together at the Olympics and wrote each other letters after the Olympics were done. Owens said, "The last letter I got from him was in 1939. . . . I answered right away, but my letter came back. So did the next, and the one after. . . . Finally, when [World War II] was over, I was able to get in touch with Luz's wife and find out what had happened to him."[12] Owens had not received any letters because Long was wounded in the war and had died from his injuries on July 14, 1943. Owens was saddened by the news. He later wrote, "I loved Luz Long, as much as my own brothers."[13] Today, the story of the two men's friendship remains one of the most compelling happenings in Olympic history.

Luz Long and Jesse Owens became close friends at the Olympics and continued that friendship until Long's untimely death in July 1943.

On Wednesday, August 5, Owens cruised through the semifinals of the 200 meters. The final was held less than three hours later. It was the last event of the day, with strong wind and a steady downpour of rain soaking everyone on the track, as well as the stadium's 110,000 spectators. Owens overcame the elements and breezed to victory in 20.7 seconds. His time was almost a half-second

◆◆◆◆◆◆◆◆◆◆◆◆◆◆◆◆◆◆◆◆◆◆◆

Mack Robinson

Had Mack Robinson won the Olympic 200 meters, the media would have had a field day with his interesting life story. Robinson was a junior college runner who had only been able to afford going to the Olympic trials in New York City after a businessman raised enough money to pay his way. He also was the older brother of Jackie Robinson, a hall of fame baseball player who, in 1947, became the first African American to play in the major leagues.

faster than the second-place finisher, fellow American Mack Robinson.

With the 200-meter victory, Owens's Olympics came to an end. He had won three gold medals and now was free to enjoy the rest of the Olympics as its most-popular spectator. Or so he and everyone else thought. Three days later, the American coaches called a meeting. They decided that Owens and Metcalfe, who had finished first and second in the open 100 meters, would be running on the U.S. 4 x100-meter relay team. The decision was extremely controversial. Although Owens and Metcalfe were the fastest American runners, adding them to the four-person relay team meant two people would have to be removed from it. Those two people were Marty Glickman and Sam Stoller. Glickman and Stoller also happened to be the only two Jews on the U.S. Olympic track team. Together with Foy Draper and Frank Wykoff, they had trained for the event for weeks. But the U.S. coaches reportedly were afraid Germany had some secret runners that would help them win the event. To counter this, they needed to put their best four runners in the event. Others believed this was untrue and that the U.S. coaches were playing into Hitler's anti-Jewish propaganda by not letting Glickman and Stoller run. Some even reported that the Germans had asked the United States not to embarrass them further by letting two Jews help add another gold medal.[14]

Glickman and Stoller were unhappy with the decision, which remains controversial even today. According to Glickman, Owens was unhappy, too. Glickman remembered Owens said, " . . . coach, I have won my three gold medals; I have won the races I set out to win. I've had it. I am tired. I am beat. Let Marty and Sam run. They deserve it."[15]

In the end, the team of Owens, Metcalfe, Draper, and Wykoff won the relay race with ease, crushing the Germans by some fifteen meters. With that big of a gap, the original team likely would have won easily, too. The relay was the only event both Glickman and Stoller were scheduled to compete in, so the two never achieved their dreams of running in the Olympics.

The relay win gave Owens his fourth gold medal of the Olympics. In each of Owens's four events, he had set a new Olympic record. His Olympics were indeed finished

Leni Riefenstahl

As Jesse Owens was breaking records and raking in gold medals, the crew of German filmmaker Leni Riefenstahl was recording every moment of it. A year before the Olympics, Riefenstahl had become famous for her film *Triumph of the Will*, which documented the rise of Germany's Nazi Party. At the 1936 Olympics, she used several cameras to document the games with the goal of turning the footage into a feature film after the games were over. In the end, Riefenstahl used so much film that she needed two years to finish the project. But when it was released in 1938, *Olympia* won Riefenstahl much praise and many awards, particularly for her use of innovative techniques to capture video footage. She even had her cameramen wear roller skates so they could capture movement. *Olympia* features now-famous footage of Owens's accomplishments as well as footage showing Hitler's frustration over the victories.

Members of the U.S. Olympic Track and Field Team at their Olympic Village headquarters, from left to right: (top row) Marty Glickman, Gene Venzke, Albert J. Mangin, Foy Draper, Forrest G. Towns, (bottom row) Cornelius Johnson, Jesse Owens, and Glen Hardin. The team won several gold medals during the games.

this time. But, at only twenty-two years old, it was likely he would return to compete in the 1940 games, when he would be twenty-six. It appeared as though many more gold medals would be in Owens's future.

The 1936 Olympics came to a finish on August 16, with a closing ceremony that ended with the words "THE LAST SHOT IS FIRED" pasted across Olympic Stadium's huge scoreboard. The Olympics had helped Hitler accomplish many of his goals. Those who attended the games returned to their respective countries and talked about how spectacular Germany was. And it had been brilliant. The host country won eighty-nine medals, thirty-three of them gold. By comparison, the United States team left Berlin with just fifty-six medals, twenty-four of them gold. Owens left the country with four of those gold medals, having placed a large symbolic crack in Hitler's ideals of a "master race."

Struggling to Survive

fter his Olympic conquest, Owens and several more of America's top athletes competed in some exhibition track meets in other parts of Europe. Tens of thousands of people came to each event. They wanted a chance to see in person those champion American athletes they had heard and read so much about. At most of these events, Owens was the main attraction. Everyone wanted to see the record breaker. But Owens was tired and wanted to return home to his family in the United States. So when it came time for him to travel to Stockholm, Sweden, for a meet, he refused to go. He said, "All I know is that I want to get back to my family. . . . I'll be the gladdest man in the world to get there, believe me. All this ballyhoo is getting on my nerves."[1]

The Amateur Athletic Union withdrew Owens from all its events and stripped him of his amateur status for failing to go to Sweden to compete. Owens and his college coach, Larry Snyder, felt that was unfair. Snyder had paid his way to attend the Olympics and he had been traveling with Owens to his post-Olympic meets in Europe. Snyder and Owens argued that the AAU treated athletes poorly, working them to the bone so the organization could make money, but not giving any of it to the athletes. On the plane ride to one meet, Owens discovered that he did not have any money, and a fellow passenger had to buy him a glass of milk and a sandwich.[2] Owens said, "This track business is becoming one of the great rackets in the world. It doesn't mean a thing to us athletes. The AAU gets the money. . . . A fellow desires something for himself."[3] It seemed to be a small request for someone who had done so much for his country.

> "This track business is becoming one of the great rackets in the world."

Owens had been young enough in his first go-round in 1936 that it was not unreasonable to believe he could return to the Olympics in 1940, and possibly even 1944, if he could somehow get his amateur status reinstated. As it turned out, World War II forced the cancellation of the Olympics for both those years. In an additional slap in the face, the AAU did not even select Owens as its athlete of the year in 1936. There was no disputing that he was the best athlete in the world. But the organization gave the Sullivan Memorial Award to Glenn Morris, the winner of the gold medal in the Olympic decathlon.

———◦◦◦———

Still, it appeared there would be a great deal of that "something" Owens desired waiting back home for him. After his Olympic victories, Owens had received many job offers that would make him a lot of money. Entertainer Eddie Cantor offered him $40,000 to perform as part of his act for ten weeks. A California orchestra offered him $25,000 to introduce its show for ten weeks. Snyder even hinted that there were bigger offers out there for his star athlete. They were in the United States, so he and Owens hopped aboard the *Queen Mary* from London to travel back across the Atlantic Ocean to pursue them.

Owens was given a hero's welcome when he arrived in New York a few days later. A large crowd greeted his ship with cheers and well wishes. Even his wife, Ruth, and his family were in town to take part in the celebration. At one point, the famous black tap dancer and actor Bill "Bojangles" Robinson took Owens aside and offered him advice on what to do next. Robinson knew that even as an Olympic hero, Owens still would have trouble finding good work as a black man in the United States. Owens even experienced America's racist ways during his own celebration. On his way to a reception being held in his honor at New York's famed Waldorf-Astoria Hotel, Owens was forced to ride the freight elevator instead of the elevator normally used by guests.[4] Many historians have reported that Owens's parents had a hard time finding a hotel in New York City that would allow them to rent a room. Owens later said, "When I came back [from Berlin],

Bill "Bojangles" Robinson offered Jesse Owens advice about
what to do with his career upon his return to the United States
after the Olympics. Robinson (left) and Owens rehearse
with several dancers for a performance in September 1936.

after all the stories about Hitler and his 'snub,' I came back
to my native country and I couldn't ride in the front of
the bus. I had to go to the back door. I couldn't live where
I wanted. I wasn't invited to shake hands with Hitler, but I
wasn't invited to the White House to shake hands with the
president, either."[5]

After a few days of celebrating in the big city, Owens and his family took a train to Cleveland. Owens was treated to an enormous parade in his hometown, just as he would be in New York City on September 3, when Owens's Olympic teammates returned from Berlin. After some rest and relaxation with his family, Owens had to decide what he should do next. He said, " . . . we couldn't afford shoes or furniture. There were four gold medals on the broken-down dresser in our bedroom, an oak tree next to the closet, and no money in my wallet."[6]

Those facts made Owens's decision easier than it may otherwise have been. He decided to take advantage of all the offers he had coming in and signed a contract with entertainment agent Marty Forkins, who also worked with Bojangles Robinson. Doing this meant he definitely would lose his eligibility to run amateur races. His college running career would be over. Owens seemed to have little problem with that. He figured he could get his college degree later. He was one of the most popular people in the world right now. He needed to take advantage of that to put food on his family's table.

Unfortunately, many of the offers Owens had received turned out to be nothing more than publicity stunts for those making them. Owens never performed with Eddie Cantor or the California orchestra. After spending six months in New York with Bojangles Robinson, he returned to Cleveland and took a job as a playground instructor for thirty dollars a week.

Jesse Owens rides in the back of a car during a parade in New York City honoring Owens and his teammates after the 1936 Olympics.

An Olympic champion of today of any race would have no problem making a living after returning to the United States. One who had won four gold medals would easily find product endorsement deals worth millions of dollars and speaking engagements worth thousands. But those lucrative deals were not available in Owens's day. He did get paid to make some speeches and endorse some products. For a short while, Owens made a decent amount of money doing so. He had enough to buy a house for himself and one for his parents. He bought a new car for his high school coach, Charles Riley. But Owens's money did not last long. Soon, he had to look for other ways to make a living. Several of them were considered degrading.

One such incident happened in Havana, Cuba, on the day after Christmas in 1936. Promoters had arranged for Owens to run an exhibition race against Cuba's fastest runner, Conrado Rodriguez, during halftime of a soccer match. When Rodriguez decided at the last minute not to go through with the race, promoters came up with another idea. They would have Owens run against a thorough-bred racehorse. Owens said he was bothered by the offer but decided to go through with it because he needed the money. He said, "I didn't know how I was going to beat a racehorse, though. Everyone realizes that a good thoroughbred can run at least twice as fast as a man."[7]

Owens was given a 40-yard head start in the race and easily beat the horse. He described how he did it in his autobiography. He wrote, "I realized that horses start much slower with a gun than when they come out of a racetrack gate. . . . I turned on all the speed I could, and it was lucky I did. . . . I was sure I would lose that first time. The closer I came to the finish line, the louder those hoofbeats became."[8] The horse was gaining on him in the end, but Owens still beat the animal. Owens was paid $2,000 for the race. Some six decades later, another banned black sprinter, Ben Johnson, also took to a racetrack. Johnson competed against two horses, and a race car. Both horses beat Johnson, but the sprinter did beat the car.

Jesse Owens runs against a racehorse in Havana, Cuba, in 1936. Owens received a head start and defeated the horse in the race.

Owens also raced against several humans, as well, including star baseball players and heavyweight boxing champion Joe Louis.[9] For a while, Owens led a professional basketball team called the Olympians. Years later, he also toured with the well-known Harlem Globetrotters basketball team.

Owens's most-lucrative post-Olympics contract came in 1937, when he reportedly was paid $100,000 to lead a twelve-piece black touring band. Owens was not particularly musically inclined, but he took the job anyway. This also was mostly a publicity stunt, and Owens knew it would not be anything more than a short-time job. He said, "Well, I couldn't play an instrument. I'd just stand

◆◆◆◆◆◆◆◆◆◆◆◆◆◆◆◆◆◆◆◆◆◆◆◆◆

Joe Louis

Because they shared so much in common, Jesse Owens and American boxing legend Joe Louis likely will forever be linked in history. Both men were born to parents who were black sharecroppers from Alabama. Both men overcame prejudice to become the best athlete in his particular sport, becoming world famous and breaking down racial barriers in the process. Both men were the same age and also had their now-infamous battles against German sports champions: Owens against Luz Long and Louis against a fellow-heavyweight named Max Schmeling. After they met, Louis and Owens became lifelong friends. Even their lives after sport paralleled one another. Both men had financial problems and continued to battle racism in their own country. Louis died in 1981 at the age of sixty-six.

up front and announce the numbers. They had me sing a little, but that was a horrible mistake. I can't carry a tune in a bucket. We played black theaters and nightclubs all over hell. One-nighters. Apollo Theater in Harlem and the Earle Theater in Philly—That was big time for blacks."[10]

By the spring of 1937, Owens needed a job with long-term security more than ever. On October 5, Ruth gave birth to the couple's second child, Beverly. Now there were four mouths to feed in the Owens household. And bills were coming due on the major purchases he had made. Part-time jobs were not going to cut it.

In 1938, Owens became a part-owner of a chain of dry-cleaning stores called the Jesse Owens Dry Cleaning Company. The new business failed within a year, leaving Owens deep in debt when it did. By this point, the Internal Revenue Service (IRS) had sued Owens for not paying taxes on money he had earned in 1936. The suit forced Owens to declare bankruptcy. A happy moment, however, came on April 19, 1939, when Ruth gave birth to the couple's third child, Marlene.

Owens's personal life took some big hits after the dry-cleaning business folded. First, his mother died in March 1940. Just a few months later, his father died. Both their lives had ended in Cleveland, the city they had traveled to decades earlier in search of a better life.

Owens was twenty-seven years old in 1940 and living in Columbus, Ohio. He had moved his family there so he could finish college at Ohio State University. He decided it was time to do something to help ensure financial stability for the rest of his life. To pay for tuition, Owens helped Larry Snyder coach the track team. But, once again, Owens never made it to graduation. His grades were as poor as they had been the first go-round at the school. At the end of 1941, Owens quit college for the second and final time.

The United States officially entered World War II in December 1941. Owens was not drafted into the military because he was the head of a household and he had to provide for his family. So the government gave Owens a job overseeing a national fitness program to help Americans get in shape. The job lasted a year, then Owens went to work for the Ford Motor Company to work with all its minority employees. For that job, Owens, Ruth, and their three daughters moved to Detroit, Michigan. The job with Ford lasted longer than any other Owens had held.

> At the end of 1941, Owens quit college for the second and final time.

Shortly after the war ended in 1945, Owens was let go from his job at Ford. He then started a sporting goods store in Detroit that did not last long.

Owens moved his family to Chicago in 1949 and started his own public relations agency called Owens, West & Associates. As with many of his jobs over the years, this job also required Owens to travel frequently, leaving Ruth and his children at home. Over the years, Ruth often said her husband made her feel like she was more of a date than a wife.[11] One author wrote that when the couple did go out together to events in Chicago, Ruth was "shocked and frightened" by the types of women she ran into.[12] They were outgoing and social, exactly the opposite of the shy Ruth. The women acted like Ruth

Jesse Owens was the head of a national fitness program during World War II. In this photo, he talks to children at a swimming pool.

did not exist, and they flirted with her husband at every opportunity.[13] Ruth trusted her husband not to let the flirting get out of hand. She said, "You do what you want to do, but respect me and respect the girls. That's all I ask."[14] Whether he always stayed faithful to his childhood sweetheart has been a subject of debate.

As a father, historians say Owens was distant with his children, a result of both his personality and the large amounts of time he spent away from home. Based on his research—which included an interview with Owens's daughter, Gloria—biographer William J. Baker surmised,

Owens and World War II

Although Jesse Owens never was part of the more than one million black Americans who fought for the United States during World War II, he did help his country in another way. When the director of the Office of Civilian Defense asked him to lead the black portion of a new program aimed at getting Americans in shape, Owens jumped at the chance. In that job, he traveled from city to city conducting clinics on physical fitness and giving pro-war speeches.

"Never did [Owens] playfully touch or hug his daughters, even in the privacy of his own home. [The daughters] all remember him as a 'Victorian-type' father who shyly held himself aloof, demanding of them proper dress and speech, respectable behavior, and obedience to paternal commands."[15]

In 1950, the Associated Press news organization named Owens the greatest athlete of the past fifty years. Though he had not run an officially sanctioned race in fourteen years, Owens's amazing accomplishments on the track in 1935 and 1936 were still remembered for the spectacular feats they were.

Chapter 7

End of
the Race

E ven as the years continued to pass, the general public never forgot Owens's accomplishments in the 1936 Olympics. He was still best known as a champion athlete, and that reputation is what continually afforded him opportunities to make money. Most of the jobs he received during his life were a direct result of his athletic success.

Beginning in 1954, Owens was appointed by the governor of Illinois to lead the Illinois State Athletic Commission. In that job, Owens preached the benefit of athletics to at-risk youth and others. In the mid-1950s, Owens held a similar role with the United States government, serving as a goodwill ambassador. Owens toured across the world to promote the benefits of athletics and the positive benefits of living in a democratic society like the United States. For two months, he traveled to such countries as India, Malaysia, and the Philippines.

In the Philippines on November 22, 1955, Owens tossed on his shorts and his running shoes and ran a 100-yard race against the country's five best sprinters. The still-active forty-two-year-old Owens whipped them all, running the 100 yards in an amazing time of 9.9 seconds.[1] Then, Owens spoke to the crowd of more than twenty thousand people who had gathered to hear him speak. He said, "Some of you young athletes have great potential. Yet success is not easily achieved. Be prepared for sacrifice. Work hard. Take instruction. . . . There is no shortcut to the ultimate goal."[2] The inspirational words were nearly identical to those Coach Charles Riley had said to Owens a quarter-century earlier: *Train for four years from next Friday.* Always be thinking about the future. They were words Owens had followed his entire life.

> "Be prepared for sacrifice. Work hard. Take instruction. . . . There is no shortcut to the ultimate goal."

During that life, it seemed whenever Owens would prosper, a setback soon would follow. In 1956, the head of the Federal Bureau of Investigation (FBI), J. Edgar Hoover, ordered the agency to look into all aspects of Owens's life. The reasons given for the investigation vary.

Jesse Owens (third from left by the water) speaks to a group
of children during his visit to the Philippines in 1955.

Some historians believe Hoover ordered it to make sure
Owens was not plotting against the U.S. government.
Others believe the FBI's explanation, which was that
Owens was being considered for a high-profile government job and needed to be investigated for it. The FBI also
had investigated Owens three years earlier. Both times,
they found he was doing nothing wrong. His friends and
associates all talked about what a nice, classy, and honest
man he was.

END OF THE RACE

Shortly after the second FBI investigation, Owens traveled to Melbourne, Australia, as President Dwight D. Eisenhower's personal representative at the 1956 Olympic Games. It had been twenty years since Owens had performed at the games. Owens also attended the 1960 Olympic Games in Rome, Italy. It was there that his last world record fell when American Ralph Boston broke Owens's long-standing long-jump record. Owens later wrote fondly of the Rome event: " . . . the Olympiad of 1960 was somehow the most exciting of all. Because that was when the last of my records—the broad jump—was finally broken. One by one my sprint marks had been erased as athletes got better and better. But somehow my broad jump record had remained."[3]

Much had happened in the more than twenty-five years since Owens had set that long-jump record. His daughters had all grown and left the house. The oldest, Gloria, had graduated from her dad's alma mater, Ohio State University, in 1953. In 1961, Marlene also graduated from Ohio State. Like her father, Marlene made it into the Ohio State University history books. In 1960, she was chosen to be the school's first black homecoming queen, and her father was the one selected to crown her in front of 83,000 people. Owens's daughter Beverly eloped and married a school principal named Donald Prather.

In 1960, Owens was honored on *This Is Your Life*, a TV show where friends and family of guests share stories about their experiences with the person being featured.

Ralph Boston competes in the long jump finals at the
Rome Olympics on September 2, 1960. Jesse Owens watched
Boston break his long-jump world record at the games.

Jesse Owens Returns to Berlin

In 1951, Jesse Owens returned to Berlin, the site of his historic Olympic conquest. He was honored by eighty thousand people in the same stadium where he had won four gold medals fifteen years earlier. In 1964, a documentary film about his return trip to Berlin was produced. It was called *Jesse Owens Returns to Berlin*. The forty-six-minute movie featured footage from Owens's 1936 Olympic triumph as well as a new interview with Owens filmed inside the stadium. In the film, Owens explained how he was greeted on his return trip to the country. He said, "I looked into the stands and everyone was on their feet. Finally, the mayor of West Berlin greeted me. Then he said, 'Jesse Owens, fifteen years ago, Hitler would not greet you or shake your hand. I will try to make up for it today by taking both of them.' . . . The cheers are with me today."[4]

Among those talking about Owens was his old coach and mentor, Charles Riley. It was the first time Riley had seen his star pupil in fourteen years. Life and distance had kept them apart. As his star pupil traveled the world reaping the rewards of the seed he had cultivated, Riley rested in a Florida retirement home. The TV show meeting turned out to be the last time Owens ever saw his "Pop." Riley died later that year.

In 1965, Owens was accused of failing to file income tax returns from 1959 to 1962. He was found guilty of the charges and ordered to pay a $3,000 fine.[5] The judge had been lenient on Owens. Owens could have received the maximum penalty: a $40,000 fine and four years in prison.[6] Court documents showed that during the four years he had not filed a tax return, Owens had made only $59,000, less than $20,000 a year.[7] It was not a horribly low amount at the time, but neither was it a large sum for someone so famous. The year he was accused, Owens was working as the running coach for the New York Mets baseball team.

Owens continued to earn his money in a variety of ways. He was a spokesperson for several corporations, including Quaker Oats, Johnson & Johnson, and Ford Motor Company, his former employer in Detroit. He also continued working for the government as a goodwill ambassador, attending every Olympic Games.

Of all the games he attended, his role in the 1968 Olympics in Mexico City—except possibly the ones he participated in—proved to be most controversial. The issue was with Owens's refusal to support the actions of two of America's top Olympic sprinters, Tommie Smith and John Carlos, teammates at San Jose State University in California. Both Smith and Carlos were African American and had considered boycotting the Olympics as a way of protesting what they believed was America's mistreatment of blacks. America was in the middle of a civil rights movement, when African Americans were fighting for equality.

The boycott never happened, but the men decided to show they stood alongside their fellow blacks. African Americans still were suffering injustices in the United States. After Smith finished first and Carlos third in the Olympic 200-meter race, the men decided that they would hold a silent, but very noticeable, protest. Both men took to the awards podium wearing black socks but without shoes, which was meant to symbolize black poverty in the United States. As the United States' national anthem played throughout the stadium, Smith closed his black-gloved fist and raised his right arm—signifying black power. Carlos raised his left arm in a symbol of black unity. He, too, was wearing a black glove on his closed fist. Both men bowed their heads as they made their gestures. Smith wore a black scarf around his neck to represent black pride. Even the second-place finisher, a white Australian named Peter Norman, showed his support for the black athletes. Norman wore a badge on his track jacket for an organization that had

> America was in the middle of a civil rights movement, when African Americans were fighting for equality.

Tommie Smith (center) and John Carlos (right) raise their fists in protest during the national anthem after receiving medals in the 200-meter race on October 16, 1968. The American runners were protesting the treatment of African Americans in the United States.

helped initiate the protest. Many Americans stood behind what Smith and Carlos had done. Others found it disgraceful, especially in a place like the Olympics, where politics were supposed to be left at the door.

Owens, who had battled racism throughout his life, stepped in. He met with the entire track team the day after Smith and Carlos made their silent statement. Owens knew the two runners were going to be expelled for their actions. Twenty-two years earlier, Owens had experienced that expulsion firsthand. He knew what it did to his career and what it likely would do to these two runners. Owens wanted to stop that from happening by talking to the men, possibly getting them to apologize. The meeting was hopeless. Smith and Carlos wanted nothing to do with Owens. Owens later wrote, "I had hopes they'd be reasonable . . . [but] Carlos lost his cool right away. . . . 'It don't make no difference what I say or do,' Carlos would keep repeating. 'I'm lower than dirt, man. I'm black.'"[8] Refusing to apologize, Smith and Carlos were suspended from the team and were not allowed to enter the Olympic Village. They were sent back to the United States, where they suffered for their decision. Some people were so angry that they even threatened to kill the two men.

After the Olympics, Owens returned to the United States, where he also faced some criticism for his actions in Mexico City. Many called him an "Uncle Tom"—a derogatory term used to describe a black man who is thought to favor white men over blacks. In 1970, Owens

> "You see, black *isn't* beautiful. *White* isn't beautiful. Skin-deep is *never* beautiful."

responded by writing a book called *Blackthink: My Life as a Black Man and White Man*. The book offered Owens's views of the racial crisis in the United States, including how he felt that "blackthink"—pro-black, anti-white beliefs—had no place in modern society. The book was Owens's response to the Mexico City issue and became highly controversial. For the first time in depth, America got to see where perhaps its greatest black athlete of all time stood on the issue of race relations. The book showed how strongly Owens was against the black militant efforts taking place at the time. A passage toward the end of the book summed up Owens's feelings on racial issues. It read, "You see, black *isn't* beautiful. *White* isn't beautiful. Skin-deep is *never* beautiful."[9]

Owens took a lot of heat for writing *Blackthink*. During his life, Owens also authored other, less-controversial books, including *The Jesse Owens Story*, *I Have Changed*, and *Jesse: A Spiritual Autobiography*.

As he always did, Owens survived the scandal and moved on with his life. In 1972, he received an honorary doctor of athletic arts degree from Ohio State University. In 1974, he was inducted into the U.S.A. Track and Field Hall of Fame. Two years later, President Gerald R. Ford awarded Owens the Presidential Medal of Freedom.

Jesse Owens pictured during graduation ceremonies at
Ohio State University in 1972. Owens received an honorary
doctor of athletic arts degree from the university.

The award is considered the highest honor a civilian can receive. President Ford said he had been among the crowd at Ferry Field in May 1935 at Ann Arbor, Michigan. It was the day Owens had set three world records in less than an hour. At the Medal of Freedom awards ceremony at the White House in August 1976, Ford talked about the 1936 Olympics and said, "Five black American athletes won eight gold medals in track and field. One American athlete in particular proved that excellence knows no racial or political limits. That man is Jesse Owens. . . . He personally achieved what no statesman, journalist, or general achieved at that time—he forced Adolph [sic] Hitler to leave the stadium rather than acknowledge the superb victories of a black American."[10]

> "For two days and two nights I lay there, on the brink of death."

By the time he received the honor, Owens finally had begun to slow down. His health played a big role in that. In 1970, he had fallen ill with a severe case of pneumonia. Now fifty-seven years old, Owens nearly died from the same sickness he had fought off so many times as a child. Owens later described his stay in a Chicago hospital. He said, " . . . the coughing came over me worse than ever, and by evening I could hardly breathe. . . . My temperature was going higher and I felt weaker than I ever had before. . . . For two days and two nights I lay there, on the brink of death."[11]

END OF THE RACE

Owens recovered. But Ruth Owens finally convinced her husband to take it a little easier. In 1972, the couple moved from the big city of Chicago to the slower-paced city of Phoenix, Arizona. Even then, Owens continued to travel to speaking engagements across the country. He still was in high demand. Everyone—from private functions to schools—wanted him to come to their events. Owens did so as frequently as possible. It seemed nothing could stop Owens from his passion for public speaking, entertaining crowds with his well-rehearsed, inspirational speeches. Then, near the end of 1979, something did. It was lung cancer.

Throughout the years and despite his athletic training, Owens had smoked a pack of cigarettes per day. Owens fought the cancer with the same enthusiasm he had applied to every battle he had faced in his life. But Owens lost this battle on March 31, 1980, when he died in a hospital in Tucson, Arizona, at age sixty-six. As she had been for most of his life, his wife, Ruth, was right by his side.

Until the day he died, Owens continued to fight for what he believed to be right. Shortly before his death, he even asked President Jimmy Carter to rethink the plans he had made to boycott the 1980 Olympic Games. The Soviet Union recently had invaded Afghanistan, and most countries did not agree with that invasion. Owens tried but failed in his effort to stop the boycott. The United States was one of sixty-five countries that did not send teams to compete in Moscow, Russia.

Chapter 8

Legends
Never Die

More than two thousand people crammed into the University of Chicago's Rockefeller Chapel on April 4, 1980, for Jesse Owens's memorial service. They came from all walks of life to honor their fallen hero, whose body had been flown from Arizona for the service and subsequent burial. Owens's college coach, Larry Snyder, was there. So was the president of the U.S. Olympic Committee, Robert Kane, and Owens's proud family. Owens's daughter Gloria read his obituary, and several others told stories about Owens. Kane told one about a young boy who once had asked him about Owens. When Kane finished answering the boy's questions, the boy said, "Wow, what a great man, I'd give anything to have known him."[1] Later that day,

Ruth Owens (center) arrives at the funeral service for her husband on April 4, 1980, in Chicago. Many people came to the funeral to honor the fallen hero.

Owens's body was buried next to a small lake at the Oak Woods Cemetery in Chicago.

Even after his death, Owens's story continued to resonate. In 1983, he was named to the United States Olympic Hall of Fame, one of several posthumous honors that would be bestowed upon him. The following year, the road leading up to the Olympic Stadium in Berlin, Germany, was named after him, Jesse Owens Allee. It was the same year *The Jesse Owens Story*, a movie about the Olympic champion's life, was released to coincide with

◆◆◆◆◆◆◆◆◆◆◆◆◆◆◆◆◆◆◆◆◆◆◆◆◆◆

Jesse Owens's Gravestone

Jesse Owens's marble gravestone is centered between two smaller marble stones, each inscribed with the Olympic symbol of five interlocking rings. The rings represent each of the areas of the world that participate in the games: Africa, Asia, Australia, Europe, and the Americas, North and South.

Owens's gravestone reads:

Jesse Owens

Olympic Champion

1936

Athlete and humanitarian, a master of the spirit as well as the mechanics of sports. A winner who knew that winning was not everything. He showed extraordinary love for his family and friends. His achievements have shown us all the promise of America. His faith in America inspired countless others to do their best for themselves and their country.[2]

the 1984 Olympic Games, held in Los Angeles. Owens's granddaughter Gina Hemphill carried the torch into the Los Angeles Memorial Coliseum during the games's opening ceremony. In 1990, U.S. President George H. W. Bush awarded Owens a Congressional Gold Medal, a military honor.

Gina Hemphill, Jesse Owens's granddaughter, carries the Olympic torch into the Los Angeles Memorial Coliseum on July 28, 1984, during the Olympic's opening ceremony.

Several other places where Owens either lived or spent significant amounts of time now boast memorials of their own. In Danville, Alabama, just a few miles from Owens's hometown of Oakville, the Jesse Owens Memorial Park honors Owens's accomplishments and life and also offers youth a place to play and grow. There are several tributes to Owens at the park, including a museum, an eight-foot-tall bronze statue, a replica of the 1936 Olympic torch, and more. There is even a long-jump pit with the distance of Owens's record jump marked off for visitors to attempt to reach. No one ever does. More than ten thousand people attended the park's opening on June 29, 1996. A few days after the park's completion, Owens's grandson Stuart Rankin carried the Olympic torch through the park en route to Atlanta, Georgia, where the 1996 Olympic Games were held.

In 2001, a new track and field stadium opened on the campus of Ohio State University in Columbus. The 10,000-seat venue's name is Jesse Owens Memorial Stadium. Each year there, the university hosts the Jesse Owens Track Classic, a very elite meet featuring some of the best high school, college, and professional athletes in the United States. Other facilities at Ohio State are also named after Owens, including two recreation centers and a tennis center. Another tribute to Owens lies some 150 miles north in Cleveland. It is a life-sized statue of Owens located in the city's downtown Fort Huntington Park.

For the rest of her life, Ruth Owens continued her husband's charity work. With the help of her daughters and several friends, she formed the Jesse Owens Foundation in 1980, the same year Jesse Owens died. The nonprofit organization's goal is to promote the development of youth, in part by awarding college scholarships. Its Web site says it, " . . . wanted to find a way to honor the spirit of a man who strongly believed in his country and the value of its youth."[3] Ruth was chairwoman of the organization until her death in 2001, at the age of eighty-six.

> "I could never amount to Jesse Owens or do the things that he's done to help African Americans, to help the sport of track and field."
>
> —*American Olympic sprinter Tyson Gay*

Over the years, several star black athletes have been compared to Owens. Those mostly include champion American sprinters, such as Carl Lewis, Michael Johnson, and Tyson Gay. In 2008, Gay acknowledged that comparison and said, "Being compared to Jesse Owens means a lot to me. He broke down a lot of barriers. I could never amount to Jesse Owens or do the things that he's done to help African Americans, to help the sport of track and field. What he did was amazing for the world, and being compared to him is a privilege, an honor."[4] The previous year, Gay had won the Jesse Owens Award, the highest

U.S. sprinter Tyson Gay celebrates his second-place finish
in the 100-meters final during the World Athletics Championships
at the Olympic Stadium in Berlin, Germany, on August 16, 2009.
The initials "J.O." on the right side of his jersey honor
Jesse Owens. Gay received the Jesse Owens Award in 2007,
the highest honor given by U.S.A. Track and Field.

honor given by U.S.A. Track and Field. Other winners have included Lewis and Johnson, as well as Jackie Joyner-Kersee, Justin Gatlin, and Allyson Felix.

Owens's story will never stop being told. Owens's life was like a roller coaster ride. He began at the bottom as the son of a poor, black sharecropper in the American South. He rose to the top as a record-breaking athlete who helped squash the will of an evil German dictator. Then he dropped down again and struggled to find work and overcome racism in his homeland. In death, Owens has once again risen to the top. He has become a legend. And legends as grand as Jesse Owens will never die.

Chronology

1913—James Cleveland "Jesse" Owens is born on September 12 in Oakville, Alabama, to Henry and Emma Alexander Owens.

1922—Moves with his family to Cleveland, Ohio.

1928—Enrolls at Fairmount Junior High School; meets future wife, Minnie Ruth Solomon; meets future coach-mentor Charles Riley.

1930—Enrolls at East Technical High School and excels at track there.

1932—Fails to qualify for the Olympic trials; first daughter, Gloria Shirley Owens, is born August 8, to Minnie Ruth Solomon.

1933—Ties world record in 100-yard dash; enrolls at Ohio State University.

1935—Sets three world records and ties a fourth at track meet in Ann Arbor, Michigan; wins national titles in four events; marries Minnie Ruth Solomon.

1936—Qualifies for 1936 Olympics in Germany; wins four Olympic gold medals, angering German leader Adolf Hitler in the process; amateur athletic career ends; races against thoroughbred racehorse.

1937—Daughter Beverly is born in October.

CHRONOLOGY

—⊷◈◈◈⊶—

1939—Daughter Marlene is born in April.

1943—Goes to work for Ford Motor Company.

1950—Named greatest athlete of the past fifty years.

1954—Appointed to the Illinois State Athletic
Commission.

1956—FBI investigates his life.

1968—Refuses to support the protest of America's top
black sprinters at the Mexico City Olympics.

1974—Inducted into the U.S.A. Track and Field Hall of
Fame.

1976—Awarded Presidential Medal of Freedom.

1980—Dies on March 31 at age sixty-six.

Chapter Notes

Chapter 1. A Historic Triumph

1. Richard D. Mandell, *The Nazi Olympics* (New York: Macmillan Company, 1971), p. 160.

2. Lawrence N. Snyder, "My Boy Jesse," *Saturday Evening Post*, November 7, 1936, p. 15.

3. David Clay Large, *Nazi Games: The Olympics of 1936* (New York: W. W. Norton & Company, 2007), p. 233.

4. Mandell, p. 227.

5. Jesse Owens with Paul G. Neimark, *Blackthink: My Life as a Black Man and White Man* (New York: William Morrow and Company, 1970), p. 110.

6. Jeremy Schaap, *Triumph: The Untold Story of Jesse Owens and Hitler's Olympics* (New York: Houghton Mifflin, 2007), p. 193.

7. Mandell, p. 227.

Chapter 2. A Love for Running

1. William J. Baker, *Jesse Owens, An American Life* (New York: Free Press, 1986), p. 6.

2. Jesse Owens with Paul G. Neimark, *Blackthink: My Life as a Black Man and White Man* (New York: William Morrow and Company, 1970), p. 31.

3. Jesse Owens with Paul G. Neimark, *The Jesse Owens Story* (New York: G. P. Putnam's Sons, 1970), p. 15.

4. Jeremy Schaap, *Triumph: The Untold Story of Jesse Owens and Hitler's Olympics* (New York: Houghton Mifflin, 2007), p. 20.

5. Ibid., p. 18.

—⌘—

6. Owens with Neimark, *Blackthink: My Life as a Black Man and White Man*, p. 39.

7. Ibid., pp. 91–92.

8. Ibid., p. 24.

9. Owens with Neimark, *The Jesse Owens Story*, p. 36.

10. "Jesse Owens quotes," JesseOwens.info: A Jesse Owens Information Site, n.d., <http://www.jesseowens .info/quotes.html> (November 12, 2008).

11. Ibid.

12. Owens with Neimark, *The Jesse Owens Story*, p. 28.

13. Baker, p. 22.

14. "Jesse Owens—Athletic Success as a Teenager," 2010, <http://sports.jrank.org/pages/3574/Owens-Jesse-Athletic-Success-Teenager.html> (November 15, 2008).

15. Schaap, p. 23.

Chapter 3. Breaking Records

1. Jeremy Schaap, *Triumph: The Untold Story of Jesse Owens and Hitler's Olympics* (New York: Houghton Mifflin, 2007), p. 27.

2. Ibid.

3. Jesse Owens with Paul G. Neimark, *The Jesse Owens Story* (New York: G. P. Putnam's Sons, 1970), p. 40.

4. Jesse Owens with Paul G. Neimark, *Blackthink: My Life as a Black Man and White Man* (New York: William Morrow and Company, 1970), p. 94.

5. Ibid., p. 95.

6. Schaap, p. 30.

Chapter 4. Greatest Day in History

1. William J. Baker, *Jesse Owens, An American Life* (New York: Free Press, 1986), p. 34.

2. Jesse Owens with Paul G. Neimark, *Blackthink: My Life as a Black Man and White Man* (New York: William Morrow and Company, 1970), p. 17.

3. Ibid., p. 15.

4. Jesse Owens with Paul G. Neimark, *The Jesse Owens Story* (New York: G. P. Putnam's Sons, 1970), p. 45.

5. Ibid.

6. Jeremy Schaap, *Triumph: The Untold Story of Jesse Owens and Hitler's Olympics* (New York: Houghton Mifflin, 2007), p. 29.

7. R. L. Quercetani, *A World History of Track and Field Athletics, 1864–1964* (London: Oxford, 1964), p. 18.

8. Bill Eichenberger, "Exquisite Owens Stood Up to Racism," *Columbus Dispatch*, March 18, 2007, <http://www.dispatch.com/live/contentbe/dispatch/2007/03/18/20070318-D7-01.html> (November 12, 2008).

9. Owens with Neimark, *The Jesse Owens Story*, p. 59.

10. "Negroes in Nebraska," *Time*, July 15, 1935, <http://www.time.com/time/magazine/article/0,9171,748861,00.html?iid=digg_share> (January 15, 2009).

11. Schaap, p. 46.

12. "Negroes in Nebraska."

13. Frank Litsky, "Eulace Peacock Dies at 82; Track Star Was Owens Rival," *The New York Times*, December 14, 1996, <http://query.nytimes.com/gst/fullpage.html?res=9D00E0D7153EF937A25751C1A960958260> (December 12, 2008).

Chapter 5. Defusing the Dictator

1. Duff Hart-Davis, *Hitler's Games* (New York: Harper & Row, 1986), p. 229.

2. "Largest Squad in History Shoves Off for Berlin and Huge Games," United Press Release,

FrankWykoff.com, © 2002–2007, <http://frankwykoff.com/manhattan.htm> (December 14, 2008).

3. Ibid.

4. William J. Baker, *Jesse Owens, An American Life* (New York: Free Press, 1986), p. 79.

5. Jesse Owens with Paul G. Neimark, *The Jesse Owens Story* (New York: G. P. Putnam's Sons, 1970), p. 62.

6. Baker, p. 84.

7. Donald McRae, *Heroes Without a Country* (New York: HarperCollins, 2002), p. 145.

8. Christopher Hilton, *Hitler's Olympics: The 1936 Olympic Games* (Phoenix Mill, England: Sutton, 2006), p. 131.

9. Owens with Neimark, *The Jesse Owens Story*, pp. 67–68.

10. Ibid., p. 69.

11. Larry Schwartz, "Owens Pierced a Myth," ESPN.com, © 2007, <http://espn.go.com/sportscentury/features/00016393.html> (December 12, 2008).

12. Jesse Owens with Paul G. Neimark, *Blackthink: My Life as a Black Man and White Man* (New York: William Morrow and Company, 1970), p. 192.

13. Ibid.

14. Schwartz, "Owens Pierced a Myth."

15. Donald H. Harrison, "Jewish Athlete Still Bitter About Ruined Shot at Gold Medal," *San Diego Jewish Press-Heritage*, July 2, 1999, <http://www.jewishsightseeing.com/germany/berlin/olympic_stadium/19990702-glickman.htm> (January 14, 2010).

Chapter 6. Struggling to Survive

1. Jeremy Schaap, *Triumph: The Untold Story of Jesse Owens and Hitler's Olympics* (New York: Houghton Mifflin, 2007), p. 232.

2. Richard D. Mandell, *The Nazi Olympics* (New York: Macmillan Company, 1971), p. 229.

3. Schaap, p. 233.

4. Larry Schwartz, "Owens Pierced a Myth," ESPN .com, © 2007, <http://espn.go.com/sportscentury/features/00016393.html> (December 12, 2008).

5. J. Y. Smith, "Olympic Track Great Jesse Owens Is Dead at 66," *Washington Post*, April 1, 1980, p. B6.

6. Jesse Owens with Paul G. Neimark, *The Jesse Owens Story* (New York: G. P. Putnam's Sons, 1970), p. 77.

7. Ibid., p. 80.

8. Ibid., pp. 80–81.

9. William J. Baker, *Jesse Owens, An American Life* (New York: Free Press, 1986), pp. 152–155.

10. "Jesse Owens quotes," JesseOwens.info: A Jesse Owens Information Site, n.d., <http://www.jesseowens .info/quotes.html> (November 22, 2008).

11. Donald McRae, *Heroes Without a Country* (New York: HarperCollins, 2002), p. 262.

12. Ibid., p. 263.

13. Ibid.

14. Ibid.

15. Baker, p. 186.

Chapter 7. End of the Race

1. Donald McRae, *Heroes Without a Country* (New York: HarperCollins, 2002), p. 287.

2. Ibid.

3. Jesse Owens with Paul G. Neimark, *The Jesse Owens Story* (New York: G. P. Putnam's Sons, 1970), pp. 89–90.

4. "Jesse Owens Returns to Berlin 1936 Olympics," YouTube.com, n.d., <http://www.youtube.com/watch?v= Fa5QQMH-T8E> (January 10, 2009).

—◆◇◆—

5. Trevor Jensen, "Longtime Downtown Tax Lawyer," *Chicago Tribune*, November 21, 2008, <http://articles.chicagotribune.com/2008-11-21/news/08112 00728_1_tax-plan-mr-kleinman-tax-evasion> (January 12, 2009).

6. McRae, p. 322.

7. Ibid., p. 319.

8. Jesse Owens with Paul G. Neimark, *Blackthink: My Life as a Black Man and White Man* (New York: William Morrow and Company, 1970), p. 80.

9. Ibid., p. 194.

10. John T. Woolley and Gerhard Peters, *The American Presidency Project*, © 1999–2010, <http://www.presidency.ucsb.edu/ws/?pid=6262> (January 18, 2010).

11. Owens with Neimark, *The Jesse Owens Story*, p. 94.

Chapter 8. Legends Never Die

1. The Associated Press, "2000 at Rites for Owens, Winner of 4 Gold Medals," *Boston Globe*, April 4, 1980, page number unknown.

2. "Graveyards of Chicago: Oak Woods Cemetery," Graveyards.com, © 1996–2009, <http://www.graveyards.com/IL/Cook/oakwoods/owens.html> (January 16, 2009).

3. "On the Starting Block," The Jesse Owens Foundation, © 1999–2000, <http://www.jesse-owens.org/jof.html> (November 12, 2008).

4. Joe Battaglia, "Quick and Quiet," NBCOlympics.com, July 2, 2008, <http://www.nbcolympics.com/athletes/athlete=170/news/newsid=125402.html> (January 14, 2009).

Further Reading

Baker, William J. *Jesse Owens: An American Life.* Urbana, Ill.: University of Illinois Press, 2006.

Edmondson, Jacqueline. *Jesse Owens: A Biography.* Westport, Conn.: Greenwood Press, 2008.

Gentry, Tony and Heather Lehr Wagner. *Jesse Owens, Champion Athlete.* Philadelphia: Chelsea House Publishers, 2005.

Gigliotti, Jim. *Jesse Owens: Gold Medal Hero.* New York: Sterling Publishing, 2010.

Schaap, Jeremy. *Triumph: The Untold Story of Jesse Owens and Hitler's Olympics.* New York: Houghton Mifflin, 2007.

Streissguth, Tom. *Jesse Owens.* Minneapolis, Minn.: Lerner Publications Co., 2006.

Internet Addresses

The Jesse Owens Foundation
  <http://www.jesse-owens.org>

Jesse Owens Memorial Park
  <http://www.jesseowensmuseum.org/>

Jesse Owens—Olympic Legend
  <http://www.jesseowens.com>

Index

INDEX